BERKELEY'S *PRINCIPLES OF HUMAN KNOWLEDGE*

pw – m

Continuum *Reader's Guides*

Continuum's *Reader's Guides* are clear, concise and accessible introductions to classic works of philosophy. Each book explores the major themes, historical and philosophical context and key passages of a major philosophical text, guiding the reader towards a thorough understanding of often demanding material. Ideal for undergraduate students, the guides provide an essential resource for anyone who needs to get to grips with a philosophical text.

Reader's Guides available from Continuum

Aristotle's Nicomachean Ethics – Christopher Warne
Berkeley's Principles of Human Knowledge – Alasdair Richmond
Berkeley's Three Dialogues – Aaron Garrett
Deleuze and Guattari's Capitalism and Schizophrenia –
    Ian Buchanan
Deleuze's Difference and Repetition – Joe Hughes
Descartes' Meditations – Richard Francks
Hegel's Philosophy of Right – David Rose
Heidegger's Being and Time – William Blattner
Heidegger's Later Writings – Lee Braver
Hobbes's Leviathan – Laurie M. Johnson Bagby
Hume's Dialogues Concerning Natural Religion – Andrew Pyle
Hume's Enquiry Concerning Human Understanding –
    Alan Bailey and Dan O'Brien
Kant's Critique of Pure Reason – James Luchte
Kant's Groundwork for the Metaphysics of Morals – Paul Guyer
Kuhn's The Structure of Scientific Revolutions – John Preston
Locke's Essay Concerning Human Understanding –
    William Uzgalis
Locke's Second Treatise of Government – Paul Kelly
Mill's On Liberty – Geoffrey Scarre
Mill's Utilitarianism – Henry West
Nietzsche's On the Genealogy of Morals – Daniel Conway
Plato's Republic – Luke Purshouse
Rousseau's The Social Contract – Christopher Wraight
Sartre's Being and Nothingness – Sebastian Gardner
Spinoza's Ethics – Thomas J. Cook
Wittgenstein's Tractatus Logico Philosophicus – Roger M. White

BERKELEY'S *PRINCIPLES OF HUMAN KNOWLEDGE*

A Reader's Guide

ALASDAIR RICHMOND

continuum

Continuum International Publishing Group
The Tower Building   80 Maiden Lane
11 York Road   Suite 704
London SE1 7NX   New York NY 10038

www.continuumbooks.com

British Library Cataloguing-in-Publication Data
A catalogue record for this book is available from the British Library.

ISBN-10: HB: 1-8470-6028-5
          PB: 1-8470-6029-3
ISBN-13: PB: 978-1-8470-6028-0
          HB: 978-1-8470-6029-7

Library of Congress Cataloging-in-Publication Data
Richmond, Alasdair.
Berkeley's Principles of human knowledge : a reader's guide /
Alasdair Richmond.
    p. cm.
Includes bibliographical references and index.
ISBN-13: 978-1-84706-028-0 (HB) – ISBN-13: 978-1-84706-029-7 (pbk.)
ISBN-10: 1-84706-028-5 (HB) – ISBN-10: 1-84706-029-3 (pbk.)
1. Berkeley, George, 1685–1753. Treatise concerning the principles of
human knowledge. 2. Knowledge, Theory of. 3. Idealism. I. Title.
B1334.R53 2009
121–dc22
2008035401

Typeset by Newgen Imaging Systems Pvt Ltd, Chennai, India
Printed and bound in Great Britain by MPG Books Ltd,
Bodmin, Cornwall

With affection and respect, I'd like to dedicate this book to an inspiring lecturer, supervisor and colleague: Robin Cameron, Regius Professor of Logic at the University of Aberdeen 1979–2001.

CONTENTS

PREFACE

George Berkeley (1685–1753) is an unusual philosopher, in that he was widely known among the religious, cultural (especially literary) and political worlds of his day. The key tenet of his philosophy is easy to state and (hence?) easy to misunderstand and to misrepresent. In a nutshell, Berkeley was an idealist and therefore held that everything that exists does so either by being a mind or by being presented to a mind. From this simple-enough sounding beginning, Berkeley's philosophy ramifies in a number of different directions. In the course of his major philosophical work, the *Principles of Human Knowledge*, he proceeds to try to reform our understanding of philosophy, science, language and religion. This book aims to take readers through every section of Berkeley's *Principles of Human Knowledge*, with a view to sketching Berkeley's arguments, antecedents and influence. (Some of the more notorious misunderstandings of Berkeley will also be sketched, along with some hints on how to avoid them.)

What follows is intended as a commentary on Berkeley's *Principles*, aimed primarily at undergraduate students of philosophy, and ideally should be read in close conjunction with the *Principles* itself. It is *not* intended as a stand-alone introduction to, or a 'reading' of, Berkeley's philosophical project as a whole.

The literature on Berkeley is large, and (alas) it isn't practical to refer in this book to all the interesting and worthwhile Berkeley material in existence. (So please don't feel offended by any omissions – considerations of space have forced either minimal or even non-existent references to many fine and worthwhile pieces of Berkeleyana.)

NOTE ON THE TEXT OF THE *PRINCIPLES*

The *Principles of Human Knowledge* is available in several editions, including:

- The standard text of the *Principles* appears in volume two of *The Works of George Berkeley, Bishop of Cloyne* (ed. A. A. Luce and T. E. Jessop, London, Nelson, nine volumes, 1948–57).
- Especially recommended for use with this book is the edition of the *Principles* edited by Jonathan Dancy as part of the Oxford Philosophical Texts series (Oxford University Press, 1998), and intended for undergraduate readers.
- *Principles of Human Knowledge/Three Dialogues between Hylas and Philonous*, edited, introduced and annotated by Howard Robinson (Oxford, Oxford World's Classics, 1996). A fine edition of Berkeley's two philosophical classics, including helpful analytical indexes and detailed introductions that cover key themes and historical context. Robinson's introduction is especially recommended on, for example, Berkeley's Master Argument and his anti-abstractionism. Robinson is usefully critical of Berkeley's arguments while remaining in sympathy with idealism.
- *Principles of Human Knowledge/Three Dialogues between Hylas and Philonous*, edited by Roger Woolhouse (Harmondsworth, Penguin, 1988). Slightly older than Robinson's edition but full of good editorial material – particularly on textual differences between editions of the *Principles*, and on the philosophical and theological disputes Berkeley had in mind when writing.
- Berkeley's *Philosophical Works: Including the Works on Vision* (ed. M. R. Ayers, London, Dent, 1975). Includes the *New Theory of Vision, The Principles of Human Knowledge, Three Dialogues between Hylas and Philonous, The Theory of Vision Vindicated and Explained, De Motu* (in A. A. Luce's

translation), plus the *Philosophical Commentaries* (with Berkeley's marginalia) and Berkeley's *Philosophical Correspondence* with Samuel Johnson. Although not as editorially detailed as some recent editions, Ayers' fine volume gathers all Berkeley's key philosophical texts in a well-edited form.

ABBREVIATIONS

References to Berkeley's works herein use the following abbreviations:

D   *Three Dialogues between Hylas and Philonous*, cited by page number from the standard Luce-Jessop edition (as reprinted in virtually all subsequent editions).
DM   *De Motu*, in the translation of A. A. Luce, cited by paragraph number.
NTV   *New Theory of Vision*, cited by paragraph number.
PC   *Philosophical Commentaries*, cited by paragraph number.
PHK   *Principles of Human Knowledge*, cited by paragraph number.
S   *Siris: A Chain of Philosophical Reflections and Enquiries Concerning the Virtues of Tar-Water*, cited by paragraph number.
TVV   *The Theory of Vision, Vindicated and Explained*, cited by paragraph number.

References to works by other authors herein use the following abbreviations:

Enquiry   David Hume, *An Enquiry Concerning Human Understanding* as in *Enquiries Concerning Human Understanding and Concerning the Principles of Morals* (1748), edited by L. A. Selby-Bigge and P. H. Nidditch, Oxford, Clarendon Press, 1975, cited by chapter and section.
Essay   John Locke, *An Essay Concerning Human Understanding* (1690), edited by Peter H. Nidditch, Oxford, Oxford University Press, 3rd edition, 1975, cited by book, chapter and paragraph.

ABBREVIATIONS

Search   Nicolas Malebranche, *The Search After Truth
and Elucidations of the Search After Truth* (*De la
Recherche de la Vérité*, 1674–5), edited and
translated by T. M. Lennon and P. J. Olscamp,
Cambridge, Cambridge University Press, 1977. The
Search is cited by book, chapter and section; the
Elucidations are cited by page number from Lennon
and Olscamp.

Treatise   David Hume, *A Treatise of Human Nature*,
(1739–40), edited by L. A. Selby-Bigge and revised
by P. H. Nidditch, Oxford, Clarendon, 2nd edition,
1978, cited by book, chapter and paragraph.

CHAPTER 1

CONTEXT

BIOGRAPHY

Born in Ireland's County Kilkenny on 12 March 1685, George Berkeley was raised at Dysart Castle. He attended Kilkenny College from 1696 until entering Trinity College, Dublin, on 21 March 1700. Berkeley obtained his BA from Trinity in 1704, wrote his major works there and was elected a Junior Fellow in 1707. Near his Fellowship examination, he began his *Philosophical Commentaries* (*PC*).[1] Although never meant for publication, *PC* is an indispensable guide to Berkeley's philosophical development.[2]

In 1709, Berkeley was ordained as an Anglican deacon[3] and published his first major work, the *New Theory of Vision* (*NTV*). Herein, Berkeley argues, against contemporary Cartesian optics, that distance is neither perceived through attending to the geometrical properties of vision nor perceived directly, as colour or shape are. Rather, we perceive distance indirectly by correlating certain visual appearances with tactile sensations of distance (e.g. changes in the strain felt by the eyes as the axes of vision change). Alone among Berkeley's publications, *NTV* only gestures at the mind-dependence of existence. (As *PC* attest, Berkeley believed all existence was mind-dependent long before writing *NTV* but felt it inopportune to defend full-blown idealism in a treatise on vision.)

In 1710, when only 25, Berkeley published *A Treatise Concerning the Principles of Human Knowledge – Part I* (*PHK*) (2nd edition, 1734). Although drawing on *NTV*, *PHK* offers a free-standing exposition of Berkeley's philosophy and detailed replies to objections. (*PHK* also boasts great prose – unusual in a work of philosophy.) The *PHK* we have is only the introduction and Part I of a work meant to include at least two, and possibly three, parts in all. Judging by Berkeley's correspondence with American philosopher Samuel Johnson, *PHK* Part II was drafted but the manuscript was later lost and no copy was ever made (*Works*, Luce-Jessop edition, vol. 2, p. 282). *PHK* Part II was to say more of spirit, God, morality and freedom, while Part III was to cover natural philosophy (i.e. physics) and science generally.[4] (While the preface to the 1710 edition of *PHK* alludes to a future instalment, the 1734 edition of *PHK* omits any reference to forthcoming parts.)

In 1712, Berkeley published *Passive Obedience*, outlining some of his moral views and arguing that revolution is never permissible. Rather than fulfil Berkeley's hopes by displaying his support for the reigning monarchy, *Passive Obedience* was read as Jacobite in sympathies and hindered Berkeley's advancement in the church. The 'Jacobite' *Passive Obedience* reads thus: if rebellion against anointed sovereigns is sinful, then British subjects owed allegiance to James II's descendants, not the inheritors of the Glorious Revolution.[5]

In 1713, Berkeley published *Three Dialogues between Hylas and Philonous* (*D*), which advocates idealism dialectically and skilfully replies to objections. The combat's issue is foreshadowed in the combatants' names: 'Philonous' trounces 'Hylas' (from Greek: 'Lover of Spirit' and 'Matter' respectively). However, Berkeley's literary skills ensure Hylas is no mere stooge but a sympathetic, well-drawn character. *D* nowhere contradicts *PHK*, but treats more extensively of the soul and addresses further (particularly theological) criticisms.

Serving as chaplain to Lord Peterborough, Berkeley toured the Continent 1713–14. During this tour, he may have met Nicolas Malebranche, one of his main philosophical inspirations. Berkeley took a second Continental tour in 1716–21, this time as tutor to St George Ashe (son of Trinity's provost). (Later, Berkeley dated losing *PHK* Part II to this second tour.)

In 1721, Berkeley was elected Senior Fellow of Trinity and published *De Motu* (*DM*), which develops *PHK*'s philosophy of space and motion. Without foregrounding idealism, *DM* exhibits such characteristic Berkeley doctrines as the passivity of ideas and the distinction between scientific and metaphysical explanation. (*DM* was written in France in 1720 and submitted for a prize-essay competition from the French Academy. It didn't win.)

Berkeley spent much of 1724–8 in London, trying to raise funds for his St Paul's College project. (Originally meant for

Bermuda, St Paul's was to train native American and colonial candidates for the priesthood.) Berkeley secured considerable private funds for his project and was promised £20,000 by Parliament. Berkeley married Anne Foster on 17 August 1728 and set off for America in September 1728. Berkeley duly settled on Rhode Island (having decided St Paul's would do better there) and worked on *Alciphron*. *Alciphron* is a series of dialogues defending Christian mysteries against freethinkers, or 'minute philosophers', as Berkeley called them, to reduce the air of independence in the term 'free thinker'. *Alciphron* is also an important source for Berkeley's later philosophy of language and science. The probable main original of 'Alciphron' himself was Anthony Ashley Cooper, Third Earl of Shaftesbury (1671–1713), English philosopher, moralist and deist, and author of *The Characteristics of Men, Manners, Opinions, Times* (1711). The character Lysicles is probably Berkeley's profoundly unenamoured portrait of Bernard Mandeville, author of *The Fable of the Bees* (1713, enlarged 1724). Mandeville had argued for the benefit to society as a whole of certain 'private vices' and mounted a stinging attack on deists like Shaftesbury and more orthodox moralists like Berkeley alike. In early 1731, Berkeley was told Parliament's promised grant would not be paid, and returned to London that October. His next major work was *The Theory of Vision, Vindicated and Explained* (1733, *TVV*).

On 19 May 1734, Berkeley was consecrated Bishop of Cloyne at St Paul's Church, Dublin. He apparently ministered well to both Protestants and Catholics in his diocese. In 1734–5, he exchanged polemics with Newtonians over the use of infinities and fluxions in the calculus.[6] In 1744, he published *Siris* (*S*). In part, *S* extols the virtues of tar water (a cold infusion of pine tar in water) as a medical panacea and details scientific and philosophical claims for its potency. However, *S* mainly comprises philosophical stepping-stones for leading readers gradually from contemplating Nature's wonders, to God as their author.[7] (Somewhat surprisingly, *S* was Berkeley's best-selling work in his lifetime.)

Apart from addressing the Irish House of Lords in Dublin in 1737 and visiting Kilkenny relatives in 1750, Berkeley remained in Cloyne for much of the remainder of his life. However, in August 1752, the Berkeley family moved to Oxford, largely so that Berkeley could oversee his son George's education. Berkeley died in Oxford on 14 January 1753. Perhaps fearing premature burial, Berkeley specified in his will that his body should stay unburied for at least five days after death, even until it 'grow offensive by the cadaverous smell' (see Luce (1945), p. 21, fn. 1). Contrary to legends that Berkeley didn't believe in physical things, his will suggests he expected his body to survive his death, and made provision accordingly.

BERKELEY'S PHILOSOPHICAL BACKGROUND

Berkeley's principal influences were John Locke (1632–1704), Nicolas Malebranche (1638–1715) and (less extensively) René Descartes (1596–1650). Berkeley inherited an essentially Cartesian philosophical background, mediated through philosophical and scientific works by Locke, Sir Isaac Newton (1642–1727) and Robert Boyle (1627–91).

Locke

Berkeley inherited a great deal of his philosophical apparatus from Locke, and shows many debts to Locke's *Essay*. For Locke and Berkeley, 'idea' covers not only concepts but all sensible phenomena of consciousness and anything that can be an object of thought. (So besides 'ideas' including concepts, percepts or representations, we can talk of perceiving ideas of colours, smells, textures, etc.[8]) Both Locke and Berkeley thought we are only *directly* aware of our own ideas.[9] However, while Locke believed our ideas can only represent their external (material) causes, Berkeley rejected such materialist representationalism and held that perception can acquaint us with physical objects themselves. For Berkeley, physical objects are nothing but assemblages of sensible ideas. (Berkeley also thought that material causation was impossible and that ideas couldn't resemble or represent causes in any case.)

Locke and Berkeley differed over substance's nature and what kinds of substance exist. Berkeley believed in mental substance (and no other); Locke was basically a dualist but agnostic about substance in general. Locke was not sure we could distinguish substances from their attributes or effects: 'So that of *Substance*, we have no *Idea* of what it is, but only a confused obscure one of what it does' (*Essay* II/xiii/19). Given the number and variety of ideas of substance, and possible ways of ordering them, we 'therefore cannot chuse but have different *Ideas* of the same Substance, and therefore make the signification of its common Name very various and uncertain' (*Essay* III/ix/13). Locke rejected a material God: 'For it is as impossible to conceive, that ever bare incogitative Matter should produce thinking intelligent Being, as that nothing should of it self produce Matter' (*Essay* IV/x/9). However, he did think that material mind was possible and that, for all we know, God could have created thinking matter (*Essay* IV/iii/6). Locke claimed to find it no harder to conceive that thinking could have been annexed to matter than he did to conceive how mental and physical substance could be brought into union (ibid.). Berkeley rejected mind/body dualism and held that thinking matter was an incoherent notion.

A key difference between Locke and Berkeley concerns abstract ideas. Berkeley thought that (1) abstract general ideas were contradictory assemblies of properties but that (2) Locke believed all language-using beings must use abstract general ideas.[10] In Berkeley's view, a Lockean abstract idea was an intrinsically general idea fitted to resemble and represent all members of a certain class of entities, and that Locke thought creating an abstract idea involved taking a particular idea and stripping away whatever made it particular. Berkeley thought this process would instead result in a mass of contradictions – as though the abstract idea of a triangle was a particular triangle-idea that was simultaneously isosceles, equilateral and scalene. Berkeley also thought Lockean abstraction was impossible because it implied the separation of qualities that can't actually be dissociated (e.g. colour and visual extension). However, it seems likely Locke and Berkeley both thought abstract ideas were merely formed through selective attention to particular ideas.[11] (Berkeley seems to have credited himself with an insight about abstract ideas that was really Locke's.)

Berkeley did allowed abstraction and general ideas, but held that we can only consider in abstraction those properties that can actually exist separately. Given a red apple, I can successfully abstract the ideas of redness and applehood. However, I can do so only because these properties can exist apart (e.g. in non-red apples and red non-apples). However, if we cannot conceive of properties existing separately then those properties cannot exist separately. (Appealing to our imaginative faculties as a test of ontological possibility is a recurring feature of Berkeley's way of arguing.)

Locke, Boyle and other Newtonians, accepted *corpuscularianism*. Corpuscularians thought the physical world comprised enduring material particles interacting in mechanical ways. Such particles were mind-independent substances with causal powers of their own. Corpuscularians generally accepted a distinction between the primary and secondary qualities of objects. While Boyle coined the terms 'primary' and 'secondary' quality, Galileo (1564–1642), Descartes and Locke (e.g. *Essay* II/viii/9–26) all accepted versions of this distinction. Primary qualities include extension, shape and solidity, where secondary qualities include colour, smell and taste. The primary/secondary distinction can be variously drawn. One version claims secondary qualities are inherently subjective and depend on percipients for their existence, whereas primary qualities are objective and mind-independent. On this 'subjectivity' criterion, physical bodies possess extension and shape but only *appear* coloured or textured. Likewise, solidity and extension could exist in the complete absence of observers, whereas taste and colour exist only if perceived. (A related criterion held primary qualities were more stable and less susceptible to alterations in the percipient's sense-organs or other circumstances. On another criterion, primary qualities were held to be accessible to more than one sense, where secondary qualities could only be accessed by one sense.)

Alternatively, the 'resemblance' criterion says: primary qualities are qualitatively similar to (and can resemble) their external causes: 'the *Ideas of primary qualities of* Bodies, *are Resemblances* of them, and their Patterns do really exist in the Bodies themselves' (*Essay* II/8/15). However, secondary qualities are causal consequences of properties in external things and don't resemble their causes. Locke thought we perceive directly ideas of colour, which are the effects of causal powers possessed by non-coloured corpuscles. However, when we perceive, for example, extension, our ideas can resemble their extended corpuscular cause. Thus, Locke held that the true nature of colour is not given to us in perception and that we might always be ignorant of what colour really is in itself. Thus, inferences from the ideas we perceive to the real constitution of their causes will always involve some uncertainty: 'the Active and Passive Powers of Bodies, and their ways of operating, consisting in a Texture and Motion of Parts, which we cannot by any means come to discover: 'Tis but in very few Cases, we can be able to perceive their dependence on, or repugnance to any of those *Ideas*, which make our complex one of that sort of Things' (*Essay* IV/iii/16). According to Locke, causal powers are represented to us only indirectly, via ideas caused in the mind, and we can't know for certain the real nature of either matter or causal power. Objects have distinctive (mind-independent) collections of powers, but we should not hope to group entities by their real essences: 'A blind Man may as soon sort Things by their Colours, and he that has lost his Smell, as well distinguish a Lily and a Rose by their Odors, as by those internal Constitutions which he knows not' (*Essay* III/vi/9). Locke held Nature was potentially capable of infinite variations on existing groups of powers. Berkeley thought insisting on the mysterious nature of physical objects a great concession to scepticism and also held that, since immaterialism holds that physical objects are simply collections of ideas, immaterialism allows us full knowledge of the real essences of bodies.

Malebranche

Although thoroughly Cartesian, Malebranche was also indebted to Scholastic philosophers and St Augustine (354–430). Unlike Descartes' interactionist dualism, Malebranchean dualism followed the medieval occasionalists and denied direct mind/body interaction. Malebranche thought God is the only true cause and hence it is (strictly) idolatrous to attribute genuine causal power to merely created things. No created substances, mental or physical, can possess causal powers, hence there can be no 'secondary causes'. All non-Divine existents are only apparent or 'occasional' causes, that is, merely provide occasions for God to act. We are not even the cause of the motions of our own bodies. For us to be able to make our own limbs obey us, we would have to be able to understand the workings of the body in all its detail, and this we simply cannot do. All efficient causation resides only in God and true mind/body interaction is impossible.

Malebranche arrived at occasionalism through reflecting on God's infinite power and attributes (not in a mere *ad hoc* attempt to circumvent mind/body interaction). Suppose you stub your toe and feel pain. How are these events related? Occasionalism says: the stubbed toe doesn't literally cause your pain. Instead, the (physical) toe-stubbing is the occasion for God to produce the pain (i.e. the correct corresponding mental event). Likewise, mental events can only provide occasions for God to produce corresponding physical events.

Where Locke thought we might have to remain ignorant of the causal powers residing in matter, Malebranche denied that there could be any causal powers in matter. (In this respect Berkeley is much closer to Malebranche than to Locke.) Locke thought we must remain ignorant of the true nature of substance or colours. However, Malebranche thought our intellectual powers could grant us a perfect understanding of matter and that we can understand what a quality like colour is. Consider Malebranche's position on the primary/secondary qualities distinction: we do not grasp the nature of colour by relation to some external mechanism that causes our ideas of colour. Instead, we can grasp what colours are because colours are pro-jected onto existing things by our minds.[12] Hence we may know what colours are truly like, but at the cost of attributing prop-erties to bodies they don't have. Hence, Malebranche maintains our knowledge of extension is genuine but our perception of colours is misleading. Berkeley rejected both Locke's 'agnos-ticism' about the real nature of colours and Malebranche's projectivism about colour.[13] Berkeley thought physical objects are genuinely coloured and we perceive colours as they are.

Malebranche held that, when we truly perceive external objects, we don't do so by perceiving ideas that reside in us but by grasping ideas that reside in God. Nothing we perceive can actually resemble matter or material properties. However, through our intellectual faculties we can grasp the ideal, gen-eral forms of material substance that reside in God's mind and then 'particularise' these conceptions. In a Neoplatonic way, Malebranche thought our intellect allows us direct con-tact with God's ideas and that these ideas can be inherently general. We cannot ourselves retain the idea of, for example, extension, therefore when perceiving an extended body, we must be brought into contact with the idea of extension in God's mind.[14] Malebranche thought ideas of extension are neither modifications nor creations of the mind itself. Neither yet are ideas transmitted to us by the causal efficacy of matter. Instead, Malebranche maintains, extension is an intelligible (eternal) idea which God's intervention renders accessible to our perception.

In his lifetime, Berkeley was often taken for a Malebranchean. His denial of material causation meant his metaphysics was thought essentially Malebranche's *sans* material substance. However, Berkeley rejected this interpretation and his work shows significant divergences from Malebranche. Berkeley did not believe in Malebranchean 'intellect' or intrinsically general ideas, but held instead that all ideas are necessarily particular and acquire generality only through use. Berkeley also rejected the Malebranchean doctrines that we can be given God (or Divine ideas) directly or that we can grasp material things through grasping God's ideas of material substance (cf. *PHK* 148).

Where Berkeley was a direct realist about perception, Malebranche and Locke upheld materialist representational views of perception, that is, our perceptions connect us indirectly with (directly imperceptible) external objects through their effects. Likewise, Malebranche and Locke both held that physical objects do not depend on perception for their existence. Berkeley's immaterialism involves a rejection of both representationalism and unperceived existence. While Berkeley shared Malebranche's belief in the causal impotence of matter, his critique of matter surpasses Malebranche, and denies that matter is even possible. While Berkeley acknowledged that his own views on the inertness of matter and the role of God as sole true cause derive from Cartesian and ultimately medieval sources, he thought he was more consistent than his predecessors in removing any need for matter. Berkeley also thought he did more justice than Malebranche to what we actually mean by 'body', for example, by rejecting suggestions that body can exist 'absolutely' or outwith perception.

A kind of scepticism about the sensible world could be charged to Malebranche too. According to Malebranche, vision is systematically misleading – whether over the size of bodies, their colour, their figures, their motion, etc. Whatever we perceive is relative to the sensory organ with which we perceive it. Malebranche concluded that the existence of physical bodies is a truth of faith and not one that can be established by reason. (By contrast, Descartes thought he had proved the existence of bodies in his sixth *Meditation*.) Without Divine revelation, we would have no reason to think that the existence of physical bodies was even probable. Berkeley rejected such conclusions as too sceptical. (Cf. *PC* 800 'Malbranch in his Illustration differs widely from me He doubts of the existence of bodies I doubt not in the least of this.') Berkeley also thought that this direct involvement of God in our perceptions misconstrued the role that God plays in acting as the guarantor of the regularity of our experiences.

Berkeley further taxes Malebranche with making matter a useless postulate. Non-occasionalist materialists at least accord causal powers to matter (even if Berkeley thinks such powers are really unintelligible) and do allow matter some role in generating our perceptions. However, the occasionalist belief that matter possesses no causal powers in itself but merely provides occasions for God to ensure that our mental events correspond with happenings in a shared world, seems to leave matter with no function. God's omnipotence cannot be constrained in its choice of instruments and God could equally have chosen to circumvent the need for matter altogether. It is surely within God's power simply to cause the correct ideas in people's minds directly, without using matter as an intermediary or occasional cause. For more on Berkeley's differences with Malebranche, see *D* 214:

> He builds on the most abstract general ideas, which I entirely disclaim. He asserts an absolute external world, which I deny. He maintains that we are deceived by our senses, and know not the real natures or the true forms and figures of extended beings; of all which I hold the direct contrary. So that upon the whole there are no Principles more fundamentally opposite than his and mine.[15]

Descartes
Besides contributing to mathematics and analytic geometry, Descartes was one of the great rationalist philosophers.

According to Descartes, certainty resides in foundational truths revealed by contemplating clear and distinct ideas. The first foundational truth in the *Meditations* is the existence of the thinking self. (Often expressed, although not in the *Meditations*, as 'I think, therefore I am' or 'Cogito, ergo sum'.) Further foundational truths are that there is a God of infinite power and wisdom, who created us and furnished our minds with innate, reliable ideas. Besides regulating the senses, reason can prove that God has given us potentially reliable faculties. Thus, the senses are not the true basis of human knowledge but must have their deliverances regulated by reason's scrutiny and judgement. By contrast, Berkeley conceived knowledge in resolutely empiricist terms, insisting that not merely our knowledge of existence but existence itself must involve consciousness. However, Berkeley had several debts to Cartesian doctrines, for example, his beliefs that genuine causation is agency and that ideas are transparent to the understanding. Also, Berkeley and Descartes have similar views on the soul's immortality.[16]

Where Descartes thought our unregulated senses were untrustworthy, Berkeley thought perception acquaints us directly and indubitably with the properties of real things. For Berkeley, we can no more doubt the objects we perceive really exist than we can doubt our own existence – the existence of the perceived object is no less certain that of the perceiving self. If sensible objects exist only in so far as they are perceived, it makes no sense to ask whether or not a given sensible object exists. Cartesian doubt about the existence of sensible objects is incoherent (like asking 'Do existing things exist?').

Descartes advocated substance dualism, holding that reality comprises two utterly distinct and irreducible substances (i.e. mind and matter). The essence of mind is *consciousness* – all mental events (hoping, planning, imagining, etc.) must involve some form of awareness. The essence of matter is *extension* – subject a material object to any imaginable physical change (cutting, squashing, melting, boiling, etc.) and it will still occupy space and possess extension. These two essences are radically different in kind – extension is not conscious and consciousness is not extended. Indeed, mental substance does not possess any spatial properties at all. Furthermore, Descartes was an interactionist, that is, a dualist who believed that mental events can cause physical events, and vice versa. In contrast to Malebranche, Descartes held that a volition (e.g. wanting a coffee) can have genuine physical effects (e.g. reaching for a mug). However, interactionists found it hard to explain *how* two such radically different substances could interact. If all physical causation is mechanical push/pull interaction, how can a physical substance have effects in the spaceless realm of the mind? Likewise, how can a non-spatial mind transmit mechanical impetus to physical objects? Berkeley believed volitions could cause physical movements but thought that his philosophy avoided problems about interaction because he held that all events occurred in minds. Where only one (for Berkeley mental) substance exists, there can be no *inter*action.

In one key respect, Berkeley is much closer to Descartes than to Locke, namely over the problem of scepticism. While they differed profoundly over the nature of our sources of certainty and the role of reason in defeating scepticism, Berkeley and Descartes both took the challenge of proving sceptic-proof foundations of knowledge very seriously. Locke, on the other hand, was less concerned with sceptical challenges to, for example, our knowledge of the external world or the existence of other minds, holding that our faculties provided us with as much certainty as we needed and that it was fruitless to seek further: 'We are fitted well enough with Abilities, to provide for the Conveniences of living. . . . In this Globe of Earth allotted for our Mansion, the all-wise architect has suited our Organs, and the Bodies, that are to affect them, one to another' (*Essay* II/xxiii/12).

CHAPTER 2

OVERVIEW OF THEMES

In *PHK*, Berkeley delineates the aims and misuses of philosophy, delivers a swingeing attack on then-contemporary conceptions of matter, proposes an alternative idealist metaphysics and considers several objections to idealism. He also outlines the advantages of idealism in supporting common sense, defeating scepticism and atheism, and restoring a proper sense of our place in God's creation. (Not a bad list of jobs, given *PHK* comprises only a 25-paragraph Introduction and a 156-paragraph main text.)

All Berkeley's doctrines, whether rules for scientific practice or proofs of God's existence, are (often brilliant) variations on a single theme. Berkeley thought philosophical confusion arose because philosophers got the relationship between perception and existence all wrong, where common sense (suitably interpreted) gets it right. Perception (actual or possible) is not an accidental accompaniment to existence or merely befalls some existent things some of the time – rather, perception (or perceivability) is the same thing as existence. Although his persona Philonous claims not to be a setter-up of original notions (*D* 262), Berkeley was profoundly influential, even if his influence wasn't always what he might have wished. Berkeley's importance rests on his case that all existence is mind-independent. Thus, he was an *idealist*. He was also an *immaterialist*, denying the very possibility of matter (at least as his contemporaries conceived it). He refused to believe in any mind-independent substance which somehow caused our perceptions, but was profoundly different from anything we perceive. Berkeleyan reality is the world we perceive, not a colourless, odourless, tasteless, textureless thing beneath our perceptions.

Although Berkeley's learning and moral probity were considered exemplary by such eminences as Alexander Pope (1688–1744) and Jonathan Swift (1667–1745), *PHK* was initially dismissed. Berkeley was often categorized as a sceptic, a sophist who sought only notoriety, or a madman who needed a physician more than serious criticism.[1] Anecdotes about reactions to Berkeley from his incredulous contemporaries are legion. For instance:

> Dean Swift is reported (perhaps apocryphally) to have left him standing on the door-step when he came to call, saying that if his philosophical views were correct he should be able to come in through a closed door as easily as through an open one. . . . After all, he explicitly denied the existence of matter; he asserted that we perceive only 'our own ideas'; and what is this but to say that we are all in a dream? Why open the door if there is really no solid, impenetrable door to be opened?[2]

Another famous eighteenth-century Berkeley gibe comes from James Boswell's discussion with Dr Johnson, the great critic and lexicographer, of 6 August 1763:

> After we came out of the church, we stood talking for some time together of Bishop Berkeley's ingenious sophistry to prove the non-existence of matter, and that everything in the universe is merely ideal. I observed, that though we are satisfied his doctrine is not true, it is impossible to refute it. I never shall forget the alacrity with which Johnson answered, striking his foot with mighty force against a large stone, till he rebounded from it, 'I refute it *thus.*'[3]

Although these cartoon objections are droll, the joke is on Swift and Johnson.[4] Berkeley believed in the solidity of stones, feet, doors and clergymen's bodies. However, he didn't believe these properties could exist (*or be conceived to exist*) independently of mind. And nobody (not even Dr Johnson) ever perceives the mind-independence of solidity. Johnson's stone was perceptible throughout its flight and Boswell saw no unobservable material substratum beneath the stone's appearance.

Berkeley held all existence is in the mind, but he did not think the world is a dream. He rejected imperceptible matter but he did not deny the world of sensible objects. Far from it – Berkeley did not deny a single one of the variously touchable, visible, buzzing, smelly and tasty things we can apprehend through our senses. For Berkeley, physical objects like trees, chairs and tables are real, genuinely possess properties like solidity, extension and shape, and can continue existing whether or not any human minds perceive them. Consider a physical object, for example, a chair. What does Berkeley think a chair is made of? In a word: *ideas*. Specifically, a chair is composed of the ideas it presents to minds – tactile ideas like hardness or roughness, visual ideas of colour and shape. What we perceive of objects is what there is. Our perception is not misleading and we are not directly aware of anything but external objects themselves. For Berkeley, *external* existence is a relative thing. Objects can exist externally to any particular (finite) percipient's mind, but no object can exist outside all minds. (NB Berkeley distinguishes two kinds of minds – finite, created minds like ours and God's unique, infinite, uncreated mind.)

Corresponding to Berkeley's two categories of existent (minds and ideas), there are two corresponding ways of existing. Ideas (singly or collectively) exist by being perceived, where minds exist by perceiving. (Berkeley also allows non-human finite, created intelligences – presumably angels. Henceforth, the caveat about angels will be assumed and 'human' denotes all finite intelligences.) The mind/ideas categories are exclusive: minds are not ideas and ideas are not minds. Ideas can't perceive and minds can't be perceived. Berkeley thinks we don't literally *perceive* mind, because we can form no ideas of mind. Minds are active, perceiving beings; ideas are inert, perceived things. No passive idea can resemble or represent the active mind. (Cf. *PC* 673: 'Things are two-fold active or inactive, The Existence of Active things is to act, of inactive to be perceiv'd.')

Berkeley did not think all existence was in his own mind. Berkeley as solipsist (or what his contemporaries called an 'egoist') is very implausible. Genuine solipsists are rare, and rarer still are solipsists who produce detailed philosophical works over five decades.[5] More importantly, Berkeley insists on the existence of: (1) God as a spirit of infinite wisdom and power, (2) other finite spirits besides his own, and (3) (contrary to legend) the physical world. So we can answer 'Was Berkeley a solipsist?' with a resounding 'No'. However, even if Berkeley was no solipsist, did his philosophy imply a solipsist position he would himself have repudiated? The situation here is more complicated. Berkeley's principles do make the existence of other minds a matter of (rather shaky) inference.

Strangely enough, there is no complete consensus as to whether or not Berkeley should be classified as an idealist.[6] However, whether idealist or no, Berkeley was not the first philosopher to make mind a more fundamental ground of existence than matter – there are strong idealistic elements to be found in the philosophy of Plato and even in certain pre-Socratic philosophers. Berkeley even had at least two contemporaries who seem to have arrived at idealist or immaterialist systems quite independently – John Norris in his *An Essay towards the Theory of the Ideal or Intelligible World* (1701–4)[7] and Arthur Collier in his *Clavis Universalis* (1713). Norris appears to have become an idealist through the influence of Malebranche[8], while Collier is significant because he seems to have arrived at immaterialism without having first been schooled in Locke.[9] However, where Norris and Collier are now all but forgotten, Berkeley's idealism remains on the philosophy syllabus to this day. Berkeley developed and systematized idealism for early modern philosophy, offering a striking challenge to the very coherence of the concept of matter, and did so on strongly empiricist principles. While he may not have been the earliest among idealist philosophers, Berkeley remains one of the most systematic and significant.

THE CENTRAL PHILOSOPHICAL ARGUMENTS

1) The transparency, particularity and passivity of ideas

Berkeley maintained that all direct acquaintance is with ideas. In turn, ideas can exist only in the mind, and only in so far as they are presented to the mind. Nothing about ideas is hidden – what we experience of ideas is quite literally what there is. This transparency extends even to properties we would normally regard as epistemological or ontological. Ideas must be inherently particular and can acquire generality only through being used to stand in for many different particular ideas. (There are thus no 'abstract general ideas', in the form that Berkeley believed Locke upheld.)

Inspecting our ideas reveal no impression of efficient causation or necessary connections between them, so ideas cannot be efficient causes or possess necessary connections with each other. Ideas are inert and cannot enter into relations with other ideas without the assistance of a mind. If our ideas contain no more of active powers or efficient causality than we perceive them to have (namely, none), whatever joins ideas must operate at a level we cannot perceive. Rather than accept causal powers residing in nature, Berkeley believed that all causality was agency, properly conceived, and that all explanation terminated in God.

2) The incoherence of material substance

Berkeley held that there is no such thing as *matter* as philosophers and scientists of his day conceived it, that is, as a mind-independent and imperceptible substance that supports the qualities we perceive. While Berkeley criticizes different definitions of matter, the central idea in all cases is that matter, if there was such a thing, would be a substance whose existence depended in no way on (actual or possible) perceiving or being perceived.

Believers in material substance usually give matter a more positive characterization than simply that of a perception-independent substance. For example, matter is usually characterized as possessing qualities like extension, solidity and mass. However, in concentrating on matter's alleged perception-independence, Berkeley was not setting up a 'straw man' position – if anything, he was concentrating on the distinctive core all conceptions of matter must have in common, that is, that of a substantial existent whose existence in no way depended upon (actual or possible) presentation to consciousness. While many conceptions of matter might add properties to the core notion of imperceptible existence, it's hard to imagine a sustainable conception of matter that is pared down further than the core notion Berkeley described and (by his own lights) destroyed.

As Berkeley realized, placing the existence of extension, solidity and density inside the mind does not suffice to banish materialism. Take away extension from mind-independent existence, and presumably solidity and density must become mind-dependent too. However, even if extension, etc. must reside in the mind, matter might be a perception-independent cause (or support) of qualities like extension or shape. The possibility of matter as 'bare substratum' explains why Berkeley expends so much effort attacking matter as an imperceptible support of perceptible qualities. Berkeley must establish not only that *some* properties are mind-dependent but that *all* are. Placing, for example, extension in the mind still leaves room for mind-independent existence but if Berkeley could show that mind-independent existence is inconceivable, belief in matter must collapse.

Berkeley refers to *a priori* and *a posteriori* objections to matter in a way which does not quite match the *a priori/a posteriori* distinction as modern philosophy conceives of it (see Dancy edition of *PHK*, p. 202, fn. 49). For Berkeley, an *a priori* objection against some doctrine is a direct argument against it, that is, showing that the doctrine is incoherent or factually wrong. On the other hand, an *a posteriori* objection is an argument that the doctrine attacked has undesirable consequences. While Berkeley principally objected to matter *a priori*, he also argued *a posteriori*. He believed he had sufficiently demolished matter *a priori* that no mere *a posteriori* appeal to any explanatory advantages of matter could avail. However, he also argued that believing in matter has undesirable consequences and that the supposed explanatory advantages in postulating matter are illusory. Properly examined, matter has no explanatory value – even if (*per impossibile*) matter could be entertained as a coherent notion, belief in matter leads to ontological inflation and explanatory obscurity. Even self-proclaimed believers in matter have no idea of what they profess to believe in or what use such beliefs might be.

Berkeley issues a challenge to wavering believers in matter: try to conceive of an existing object which is not (in some sense) present to your conception *and thus* perceived by you. If you can conceive of an unconceived object, then Berkeley grants immaterialism is defeated. However, this is a concession Berkeley feels he can afford, as he thinks the postulated conception of an unconceived object is a contradiction in terms.

Nowadays, 'materialism' means the doctrine that *all* existents are material – that no non-material objects or properties exist and that mental events too are material phenomena. Contemporary materialists are substance monists, that is, believers that only one kind of substance composes all reality. Materialist substance monists have a long philosophical pedigree, for example, the Greek atomists Democritus and Epicurus (c. 460–c. 370 BCE and 341–270 BCE respectively) or Thomas Hobbes (1588–1679). (Hobbes thought even the soul and God are merely attenuated forms of matter.) However, as Berkeley's example demonstrates, there are also *idealist* substance monists, who think mental substance composes all reality. (Obviously, these two forms of monism are mutually exclusive – an idealist can't be a materialist, nor a materialist an idealist.) There are also substance dualists, who believe reality is ultimately composed of two (usually mental and material) substances. (Descartes was a notable substance dualist.) So in the modern sense, one cannot accept both Berkeleyan idealism and Hobbesian materialism, and neither can one be a materialist like Hobbes and a dualist like Descartes.

However, Berkeley uses 'materialism' in a wider sense than modern philosophers, to mean the doctrines that matter does exist or *could* exist. Where modern materialism claims all is matter, Berkeley's materialists merely think matter is an actual or possible existent, that is, that there is (or could be) such a thing as mind-independent substance. Modern materialism excludes all non-material existents but the materialism Berkeley rejected is compatible with non-material existents. So, odd as it sounds, mind/body dualists like Locke and Descartes are just as much materialists in Berkeley's sense as materialist monists like Hobbes. So Berkeley opposes not just Hobbesian 'All is matter' materialism, but also the milder doctrines that material substance does (or could) exist. As Berkeley's principal target was the conceivability of matter, he was opposed to materialism in a very strong sense. (It's hard to see how one could take a more anti-materialist stance than building one's entire philosophical project on the redundancy and outright logical impossibility of matter.)

To try to prevent confusion with modern uses of 'materialism', Luce (1945, p. 25, fn. 1) coined the term 'matterism' for the broad doctrine that there is (or could be) such a thing as material substance and suggested that 'materialism' should be reserved for the narrower doctrine that all existence is material. (Obviously any materialist is *a fortiori* a matterist as well – one cannot believe that all existence is ultimately material while denying that there is such a thing as matter.) So, in Luce's terminology:

- Democritus, Epicurus and Hobbes are both matterists and materialists.
- Descartes, Malebranche and Locke are matterists but not materialists.
- Berkeley is (obviously) neither matterist nor materialist.

Luce's 'matterism' didn't catch on, so unless stated otherwise, please assume 'materialism' is henceforth used as Berkeley used it, that is, for the doctrine that matter does (or could) exist.

CHAPTER 3

READING THE TEXT

The following aims to give a paragraph-by-paragraph break-down of Berkeley's argument at each stage. Some paragraphs can be mentioned only briefly, while some demand much more extensive exegesis, but all are worth annotating.

SECTION 1: THE PRINCIPLES – INTRODUCTION (§§1–25)

Summary
PHK's full title is a handy guide to Berkeley's aims:

> A Treatise Concerning the PRINCIPLES of *Human Know-ledge*. Wherein the Chief Causes of Error and Difficulty in the *Sciences*, with the grounds of *Scepticism*, *Atheism* and *Irreligion*, are inquired into.

One might add 'idolatry' to the list of views Berkeley found objectionable and which (he believed) materialism helped support. However, note that nowhere in *PHK*'s title-page, dedication or Introduction is *matter* mentioned. As Berkeley's letter to his friend, Sir John Percival, of 6 September 1710 (Rand, 1914, p. 82) makes clear, this omission is not accidental:

> However I imagine whatever doctrine contradicts vulgar and settled opinion had need been introduced with great caution into the world. For this reason it was I omitted all mention of the non-existence of matter in the title-page, dedication, pref-ace, and introduction, that so the notion might steal unawares on the reader, who possibly would never have meddled with such a book that he had known contained such paradoxes.[1]

Much of *PHK*'s Introduction attacks Lockean abstract ideas, as Berkeley reconstructed them. The problem of abstract ideas is that of how we derive general knowledge from contact with particular objects. Many philosophers (notably Plato, c. 428–348 BCE) addressed this problem via realism about universals. Realism about universals claims that, besides particular entities (such as chairs, tables, mountains and persons), there are also universals. Where particulars can only have one location at a time, universals can reside (completely and simultaneously) in many different particulars. Candidates for universals include *properties* (like redness or tallness) and *relations* (like 'being married to' or 'being heavier than'). The ontological status of universals has long been controversial – how can one and the same entity appear in many, spatio-temporally disjoint, places? Nominalists (such as William of Ockham, 1285–1347) reject universals, usually maintaining that the only general entities are names or classifications created by human conceptual efforts. Empiricists traditionally share nominalist suspicion of universals. Berkeley can be considered as a nominalist, but he's perhaps better described as a *particularist*, that is, one who rejects all general or abstract entities. (For example, he thought all relations depended on acts of the mind.) Berkeley thought any existing ideas must be inherently particular and cannot possibly have the properties attributed to abstract ideas by Locke. Berkeley thought Locke's account of general ideas moved intrinsic generality away from universals outside the mind and into ideas themselves. Berkeley thought perception could reveal any intrinsic properties of ideas, hence generality was the wrong sort of property for ideas to possess and that no idea could be intrinsically general in the way it could be intrinsically square or yellow.

Section by section
§1 Berkeley initially asks whether philosophy solves problems or creates them. Alas, it seems more often the former than the latter. As philosophy aims at studying wisdom or truth, philosophers ought to possess greater serenity and contentment than other folk but clearly they don't. The 'illiterate bulk' of humanity do their business untroubled by sceptical doubts, whereas those who obey a supposedly higher calling and pursue wisdom find themselves doubting things that had previously seemed clear. Philosophers seem prone to endemic sceptical doubt. Thus, anyone who undercuts scepticism will increase contentment.

Seemingly, many of Berkeley's aims are not *philosophical* at all, but rather the removal of philosophical obstacles to correct living. (In his *Meditations*, Descartes sought a reformation of metaphysics, not as end in itself, but as the prelude to restructuring the whole basis of knowledge. Cf. the famous remark from Ludwig Wittgenstein (1889–1951) that the 'ladder' of his *Tractatus* must be thrown away once climbed.[2])

§2 Does 'the obscurity of things' or the weakness of our intellectual powers create the puzzlement and confusion attendant on doing philosophy? We have few faculties and we are finite, hence it may not be so surprising that we are baffled by the apparent infinities uncovered by our senses in nature and by our reasoning.

§3 But maybe we are too lenient with ourselves if we blame our confusion on the (comparative impoverishment) of our faculties. Maybe it's how we deploy our faculties that cause trouble. Correct reasoning from correct principles should not generate confusion. God would not have made us desiring of knowledge but then left us frustrated in our search for it. Maybe our confusions are really self-generated: 'we have first raised a dust, and then complain, we cannot see'.[3]

§4 Berkeley thus aims to uncover the principles that led to philosophical confusion – an anatomy of the philosophical dust in our eyes, if you like. This endeavour will be particularly useful if we find our confusions don't derive from the objects we consider or the faculties we use, but from our using false principles. If our failings don't proceed from permanent and irredeemable features of our nature or the world, but from our own mistaken principles, then if we can replace our current false principles with new true ones, there is hope of reforming our reasoning and dispelling our confusions. Berkeley's project is an optimistic one: we can diagnose and rectify our own philosophical ills.

§5 In setting out to reform human thinking, Berkeley (rather endearingly) disclaims any claims of superiority of intellect on his own part. Many illustrious and better-sighted thinkers have preceded him but maybe myopia is a blessing here and will lead to a closer attention being paid: 'he who is short-sighted will be obliged to draw the object nearer'.

§6 To help the reader, some observations about the abuse of language are needed. At the risk of anticipating later remarks,

Berkeley emphasizes the dangers in the opinion that the mind can frame abstract (general) ideas. A novice in philosophy might think that logic and metaphysics are all about the study of such ideas, when in fact no such abstract (general) ideas as the philosophers countenance can exist.

§7 Everyone agrees the properties that something possesses cannot exist separately or in isolation. Qualities are always found mixed and blended together. However, philosophers claim the mind can consider qualities separately – as if in isolation from others. Suppose one sees an extended, coloured and moving object – Berkeley's abstractionist opponents believe that the mind can somehow resolve this compound idea into its constituents and 'frame the abstract ideas of extension, colour and motion'. However, from the exercise of this power of the mind, it does not follow that such qualities can therefore exist in isolation.

§8 The mind can also detect that particular extensions both have something in common and something that makes them particular. (Not all visual objects have the same shapes or colours but all are nonetheless extended.) It is also supposed that the mind can attend to what various extensions have in common and can thereby create the abstract idea of extension, which somehow 'is neither line, surface nor solid'. Likewise, the mind can (allegedly) form an idea of colour which reflects what all colours have in common but omits the particularity of any given colour, that is, 'an idea of colour in abstract which is neither red, nor blue, nor white, nor any other determinate colour'. Likewise, an abstract idea of motion would discount 'all particular direction and velocities' but somehow reflect whatever all the motions that can be presented to the senses have in common. Berkeley steadfastly maintains no such ideas can be formed. Any idea of extension must be an idea of a line, a surface or a solid – it cannot be all, or none, of these three. Similarly, any idea of colour must be the idea of some particular colour – it cannot be all or none of the colours at once – and any idea of motion must exemplify a determinate speed and direction.

§9 We are also told that, just as the mind can form abstract ideas of particular qualities, so it can form abstract ideas of compounds of qualities, for example, the abstract idea of 'Man'. As all men have some colour and stature, the abstract idea of

Man must include colour and stature but cannot exemplify any *particular* colour or stature.

§10 Although unable to tell whether or not others possess the faculty of creating such abstract ideas, Berkeley seems confident he does not. However, he can imagine qualities and parts of objects he has perceived being combined and divided in new ways. He can imagine a two-headed man or a centaur, for example. (Exercise for the reader: given the idea of a person with two eyes and a nose, you should be able to entertain the idea of a person with one eye and two noses. Framing the ideas of an eight-legged horse or a horse's head joined to an eagle's body shouldn't be beyond you either.)

Likewise, parts that could be separated in actuality can be separated in imagination: for example, Berkeley allows that eyes, hands and noses can all be considered in isolation from the body. However, any visual idea we entertain of, for example, a hand or eye must give that hand or eye a particular, determinate shape and colour. Likewise, the visual idea you form of a man must possess determinate colour, shape and height. However, Berkeley thinks it's impossible to form an abstract idea that lacks such particularity. No idea of motion can be abstracted from the idea of a moving body, neither can that idea of motion be neutral between fast motion or slow. So, Berkeley allows abstraction *qua* considering separately those parts or qualities of an object that can exist separately, but rejects abstraction *qua* considering separately things that cannot exist thus separated.

§11 Why do other philosophers believe in the kind of abstraction Berkeley rejects? Berkeley alludes to Locke (*Essay* II/xi/10 and 11), who claimed that abstract ideas were necessary for language-use and that the facility for generating such ideas was what distinguished humans from animals. Animals show no signs of 'making use of general signs for universal ideas', as they lack language. However, while Berkeley grants that animals can't form Lockean abstract ideas, he also thinks 'a great many of those that pass for men must be reckoned into their number'. By implication, Berkeley thinks he belongs among the animals on Locke's criterion. Certainly, Berkeley takes Locke to be claiming that it is distinctively human to use language and that the use of language in turn involves having abstract general ideas, while in turn claiming that he, that is, Berkeley, can't form any such ideas. Berkeley furthers charges Locke with holding that a word becomes general through signifying (or standing for) an abstract *general* idea. In Berkeley's reconstruction of Locke, an abstract general idea is an idea which is somehow intrinsically general. (Berkeley cites Locke here: 'Words become general, by being made the signs of general *Ideas*', *Essay* III/iii/6.) Instead, Berkeley suggests that particular ideas become general by standing 'indifferently' (i.e. without favouring one over another) for several particular ideas, rather than for a single general idea.

§12 If we attend to how it is that ideas can become general, we may also learn how words acquire general signification. Berkeley is careful to specify that he denies only *abstract* general ideas, not general ideas *per se*. Ideas become general through use, that is, 'by being made to represent or stand for all other particular ideas of the same sort'. A mathematical demonstrator draws a line on the board to illustrate the general process of bisection – of course, the line drawn must have a particular size, colour and shape but it can nonetheless become general by being used to represent all lines.

§13 Berkeley charges Locke with holding that abstract ideas are mental images which somehow combine all possible properties of the relevant particulars they represent. Berkeley cites (not entirely in context) Locke's famous passage about the creation of the abstract general idea of a triangle. Berkeley takes this abstract triangle to be a Frankensteinian creation that contrives to be equilateral, isosceles and scalene all at once:

> For example, Does it not require some pains and skill to form the *general Idea* of a *Triangle* (which is yet none of the most abstract, comprehensive, and difficult), for it must be neither Oblique, nor Rectangle, neither Equilateral, Equicrucal, nor Scalenon; but all and none of these at once. In effect, it is something imperfect, that cannot exist; an *Idea* wherein some parts of several different and inconsistent *Ideas* are put together. (*Essay* IV/vii/9)

Berkeley may be making unfair game of Locke here. Locke also thought general ideas were not general intrinsically or of their own nature but became general only through usage. In other words, an abstract idea of a quality (e.g. whiteness) will be formed by selective attention[4] to particular ideas of white things and not by somehow making an idea that simultaneously instantiates all sizes and shapes of all white objects:

> This is called ABSTRACTION, whereby *Ideas* taken from particular Beings, become general Representatives of all of the same kind; and their Names general Names, applicable to whatever exists conformable to such abstract *Ideas*. . . . Thus the same Colour being observed to day in Chalk or Snow, which the Mind yesterday received from Milk, it considers that Appearance alone, makes it a representative of all of that kind; and having given it the name *Whiteness*, it by that sound signifies the same quality wheresoever to be imagin'd or met with; and thus Universals, whether *Ideas* or terms, are made. (*Essay* II/xi/9)

In view of remarks like the above, it's not clear that Locke believed that language-use required the formation of ideas which were literally images which exemplified contradictory sets of properties. Thus, Berkeley's notion that ideas acquire generality through usage and selective attention might well have been something like Locke's idea of generality too. However, in defence of Berkeley's version of Locke, if the pains and difficulties that Locke adverts to in the creation of abstract ideas don't arise through abstract ideas being imagistically conceived, it's hard to see whence they do arise.[5] It isn't clear why the mere use of selective attention should be so stressful. Some of Locke's remarks do help to make Berkeley's misreading of him, if such it is, pardonable.

§14 Supposing we do somehow form abstract (general) ideas, Berkeley next asks when in our development it is that we manage to form them. It's granted on all sides that the creation of abstract general ideas is a laborious business and one that calls for a high degree of skill and perseverance. It seems implausible that pulling off such a demanding feat could be a necessary precondition for the mere possibility of interpersonal communication. We can't form such ideas in adulthood, because we would be aware of the process. However, it seems that no child could possess the requisite cognitive dexterity for framing abstract general ideas either. (Cf. *Essay* I/iv/2–3 on children's apparent lack of innate ideas.)

§15 Abstract general ideas seem no more useful considered as vehicles for knowledge than as prerequisites for communication. While Berkeley happily agrees that 'all knowledge and demonstration are about universal notions', he does not accept that such notions are of abstract general ideas, especially if created along Lockean lines. The universality of an idea is a relational property and a function of how that idea is used to signify other ideas. Universality is not, and cannot be, a property that is somehow intrinsic to an idea. (An idea may have intrinsically a non-relational property like being yellow or being square but it cannot *intrinsically* possess universality.) While ideas are inherently particular, they can acquire universal significance through being made to stand in for other ideas of a similar type. So, if in a mathematical demonstration of properties of the triangle, I make use of the universal idea of triangle, this universal idea is not to be conceived of as some strange hybrid that contrives to be 'neither equilateral nor scalenon nor equicrural'. Rather, the universal idea used is that of a particular triangle, which is standing in for or representing all other triangles. Thus, it is the use to which a particular idea is put that makes it universal, and not some intrinsic feature of 'universality'.

§16 Consider a demonstration of, for example, Pythagoras' Theorem. Berkeley imagines an opponent protesting: But how can I be sure that this truth applies to all triangles whatsoever if it is not demonstrated of the abstract idea of triangle? It's clear that not all triangles have exactly the same properties and therefore we should be wary of assuming that a truth demonstrated of some particular triangle must therefore hold for all. (For example, just because I have seen it demonstrated of a particular isosceles triangle that its angles sum to 180°, need it follow that this is true of all isosceles triangles, still less of all triangles?) Should we not then on Berkeley's principles have to forego all general mathematical demonstrations and instead make a particular demonstration for each of the (indefinitely many) different triangles there might be? Berkeley replies that while any demonstration must involve a particular triangle, it can still be of general significance. A demonstration that the sum of internal angles is equal to two right angles need make no reference to the particular lengths of side, or sizes of angle, of the triangle under consideration. Again, selective attention makes a particular idea capable of general representation. A particular equiangular triangle may be considered *qua* triangle without also being considered as equiangular. Likewise, we can consider the same particular under different classifications without having to invoke or to imagine abstract general ideas. (Berkeley instances considering a particular human being, Peter, as man or animal.) Not every quality we perceive in a particular must be an object of attention on every occasion on which we perceive that particular.

§17 The doctrine of abstract ideas has been uniquely prone to create metaphysical confusion. (Witness the needlessly elaborated and obscure philosophy of the Schoolmen, that is, the medieval Scholastic philosophers, of whom the greatest was St Thomas Aquinas, 1224–74.) Believing in abstract general ideas is perhaps *the* philosophical mistake, and Berkeley finds it remarkable that so much scientific and mathematical progress could have been made while their exponents remained in such philosophical confusion over fundamentals like the nature of abstraction.[6]

§18 The error about abstract ideas is (at least partly) parasitic upon a prior error about language. Partly the mistake is assuming that every name has a precise and clearly delineated meaning. In turn, only (a misuse of) reason could have made this error so widely accepted. The upholders of abstract ideas (Berkeley refers to Locke, *Essay* III/vi/9) erroneously assumed that every general name of determinate meaning must correspond to a single, determinate idea. Whereas in fact, any name can stand for a multitude of different ideas. Berkeley considers the objection that a definition must be as precise as possible and must delimit the associations of each word defined to as few ideas as possible. To which, Berkeley replies that precision in definitions is not the same as restricting the associations of the word defined to a single idea. For example, if we define a triangle as a three-sided plane figure, this definition is sufficiently precise but it does not restrict the term defined to any single idea, since it can stand indifferently for triangles of any colour, size of angle or length of side. While it is useful to keep one word annexed to a single definition, it is neither useful nor practical to limit the associations of a word to a single idea. While this last doctrine is clearly one Berkeley attributes to Locke, it's not clear though that Locke held any such thing. See, for example, Bennett (1971, p. 23), who finds no trace in Locke of the notions that a general name was a proper name or that general words must be annexed to single determinate abstract ideas in their users' minds. Here too Berkeley may be implicitly congratulating himself for throwing off a Lockean error which Locke never actually made.

§19 Language is (at least in part) a set of artificial relations between ideas, although Berkeley expressly states that language can have other functions besides reflecting associations of ideas. Likewise, he thinks not every word need stand for a single, fixed idea in order to be meaningful. Berkeley thinks that a key philosophical error is assuming that all language exists to communicate ideas, and that every meaningful symbol must stand in for a determinate idea. (Some entries in *PC* suggest Berkeley considered – only to reject – such an 'ideational' view of language pre-*PHK*. Cf. *PC* 422: 'No word to be used without an idea'.[7]) Hence, when philosophers found they could entertain no such single *particular* idea answering to all possible applications of a term like 'triangle', they concluded there must be an *abstract* general idea that was the bearer of meaning for 'triangle'. However, first, many names are in widespread use which don't always suggest determinate ideas to their hearers and secondly, ideas don't always have to arouse in us the same ideas at each and every occasion of their use.

§20 Language needn't invariably be used for communicating ideas: 'The communicating of ideas marked by words is not the chief and only end of language.' Likewise, terms can have a general signification without arousing any particular ideas in their hearer. Berkeley distinguishes several non-ideational ends that language can serve, such as 'the raising of some passion, the exciting or deterring from an action, the putting the mind in some particular disposition'. Indeed, not only need words not always arouse particular ideas in their *hearers*, some general terms need not even be accompanied by any particular ideas on the part of whoever *utters* them: 'When a Schoolman tells me

Aristotle hath said it, all I conceive he means by it, is to dispose me to embrace his opinion with all the deference and submission which custom has annexed to that name.' An utterance like that has a persuasive force, and should issue in a feeling of assent, rather than trying to convey an idea or proposition. (Here, Berkeley's distinction between the different uses language can be put to anticipates some of the distinctions later drawn by J. L. Austin.[8])

§21 Some of the difficulties that follow from mistakes about language might be avoided if we attended more to our ideas and less to words. Words have a nasty habit of misleading, or imposing upon, our understanding. (Ideas, on the other hand, are transparent to our understanding and much less prone to error – a significant premise for Berkeley.[9])

§22 Many benefits can accrue from throwing off philosophical errors derived from language. The first benefit will be a reduced susceptibility to the doctrine of abstract general ideas. Secondly, we would then have a reduced risk of getting embroiled in purely verbal disputes, which have bedevilled and impeded philosophical debate. Here and elsewhere, Berkeley is quite serious in maintaining that errors about language are a prime source of philosophical confusion. In particular, he singles out the mistake of assuming that every substantial noun (or name) must have a real existent that corresponds to it. Furthermore, he argues this error (in large part) explains the deeply mistaken belief in abstract general ideas. The worst consequence of this kind of abstractionist error has been philosophers' tendency to take seriously the notions of material substance and the belief in the possibility of absolute (non-perception-dependent) existence. (So, while it may appear to the modern reader that the attack on abstract ideas is given a disproportionate emphasis in *PHK*, Berkeley would not agree with this assessment. Although when Berkeley recast his arguments for immaterialism in *D*, the attack on abstract ideas received far less emphasis therein.) The errors arising from the doctrine of abstract ideas are particularly dangerous, because philosophers have been susceptible to them in exact proportion to their intellectual acumen. Thirdly, if we are encouraged to return to a consideration only of our own particular ideas, there will be a gain in knowledge – we are far less likely to be mistaken about the contents of our immediate experience. Indeed, attending strictly to the immediate contents of experience should make errors impossible: 'I cannot be deceived in thinking I have an idea which I have not.' Likewise, I can't be mistaken in judging whether or not two (or more) of my ideas genuinely resemble each other. Nor can I be mistaken as to what simple ideas are present in a compound idea. Without overstressing this analogy, a belief in the indubitability of the immediate contents of experience is Berkeley's foundational equivalent of the Cartesian *Cogito*, but with the significant difference that Berkeley's foundations are thoroughly empiricist ones and derived from immediate sensory experience. (By contrast, Descartes takes an altogether more rationalist foundational line, holding that the only true epistemic foundations are self-evident truths to be uncovered by the unaided reason. Descartes held that the senses are not of themselves a source of certainties and that any claims to empirical knowledge had to be ratified by the reason.)

§23 However, given his thoroughly realistic assessment of human cognitive powers and his own persuasive powers, Berkeley says all these advantages will accrue only if we could completely emancipate ourselves from errors about language, and he suspects such complete success is not to be expected. The belief in an association between every meaningful name and a corresponding determinate idea is far too deeply ingrained to be easily dislodged. However, another mistake seems to have been in play – people mistook the difficulty of retaining an idea in the mind without also retaining a corresponding substantive word associated with it, for the impossibility of forming an abstract idea. The former task (i.e. attending to our ideas without associating words with them) may be difficult but the latter task (i.e. forming abstract general ideas) is starkly nonsensical. Consequently, even those philosophers who have made (in Berkeley's view highly praiseworthy) exhortations to us to set aside our words and contemplate our ideas unadorned, have singularly failed to abide successfully by their own precepts. (It's probable Berkeley meant Locke here, who frequently inveighed against the mere linguistic disputes that Scholastic metaphysics generated. Berkeley and Locke shared a suspicion of Scholastic metaphysics and both distrusted Aristotelian explanations and the 'essential natures' such explanations postulated.[10]) However good such advice is, even its originators won't be able to follow it, so long as they believe (1) every significant word must have an idea annexed to it, and (2) every general name must signify a corresponding *'determinate, abstract idea'*.[11]

§24 However, once the above errors are identified as such, there's hope of overcoming them. Once you realize all your ideas must be particular, you won't tie yourself into knots trying to uncover the abstract general ideas that supposedly accompany the general terms you use. So one clear Berkeleyan precept is: try to get as clear a sense as you can of your ideas in their particularity, without being distracted by the words that are associated with your ideas. (Berkeley closes this section with a wonderful purple paean to the truths that lie ready to be uncovered by the above method.)

§25 Without due clarity about our ideas, and without observing the above advice to clear our understanding from the misleading associations of our language, our philosophical endeavours might be prolonged infinitely without ever yielding certainty or wisdom. So, in a final piece of advice before *PHK* proper, Berkeley suggests the reader should try to achieve the same succession of ideas in reading the text that Berkeley had in writing the text. (Presumably this means the reader ought to try to achieve the same successive steps in reasoning Berkeley underwent, rather than trying to duplicate the succession of mental images Berkeley might have had while writing. However, Berkeley's repeated insistence on attending to ideas in their particularity without being distracted by their accompanying words does make it sound as if our aim in reading *PHK* should be duplicating the succession of ideas that passed across the theatre of Berkeley's mind during *PHK*'s composition. Following a similar chain of thoughts and inferences to Berkeley's own seems both a possible and a potentially useful undertaking for his readers; duplicating the sequence of his mental images seems both harder and less profitable, even rather pointless, if it could be achieved.) If the reader attends purely to the resulting succession of 'naked, undisguised ideas', no danger of error can arise. So, suitably warned against unbridled abstraction and prepared to re-enact the sequence of Berkeley's original ideas, we are ready to tackle the main text of *PHK* (Part I).

Questions

1. Are abstract ideas the causes of so much philosophical confusion as Berkeley would have us believe?
2. Is Berkeley's account of the generation of Lockean abstract ideas a fair one?
3. Would error really be eliminated if we could only learn to attend scrupulously to our own ideas?

SECTION 2: THE PRINCIPLES – PART I (§§1–156)

THE OBJECTS OF KNOWLEDGE: IDEAS AND SPIRITS (§§1–33)

The objects and subject of knowledge: Ideas and spirit (§§1–3)

Summary

The opening paragraphs of *PHK* contain (often in a rather telescoped form) many of the later crucial stages of Berkeley's argument. For instance, Berkeley adverts early on to his view that the scope and ambitions of philosophy should be tempered by a respect for common sense; what Berkeley later calls thinking with the learned and speaking with the vulgar. Berkeley thought philosophers were often prone to overrarefied and sloppy thinking, preferring the abstract to the concrete to a dangerous degree. Thus, Berkeley's claim to uphold common sense was no idle boast or mere lip-service paid to win a hearing for an outlandish doctrine but a seriously held regard for ways of thought that had escaped philosophical infection. Common sense metaphysics accepts that what we immediately perceive are real things, not mere representations or effects of real things. However, common sense metaphysics errs in thinking objects can exist independently of perception.

On the other hand, Locke (and others) thought we don't perceive physical objects directly but perceive only ideas directly. (These ideas are supposedly caused by external objects and can copy some of their properties.) Berkeley thought materialist representationalism was correct in claiming that we immediately perceive only ideas but wrong in claiming that we directly apprehend only the effects of real things. Berkeley thus upheld direct realism about our perception of physical objects. Materialist representationalism implied the perceived world need not resemble the world as it really is and so engendered scepticism. Rejecting perceptual scepticism, Berkeley insists we can directly grasp real physical things as they are. In seeing a tree, what you directly grasp is the tree itself and not some intermediate copy that intervenes between you and the tree. Thus, you don't merely receive coloured and extended effects caused by some hypothetical, imperceptible 'real' tree. Behind the ideas percipients can acquire of sensible objects, there is no extra imperceptible somewhat that underlies and causes perceptible properties. Our perceptions can inform us directly, without mediation, of the real properties of physical objects. For Berkeley, real things are simply collections of ideas, nothing more.

Section by section

§1 First, Berkeley delineates the *objects* of knowledge. Clearly, the objects of human knowledge are ideas, and ideas in turn can be of only three kinds: ideas imprinted on the senses, ideas acquired through attending to 'the passions and operations of the mind', and ideas formed via memory or imagination. (The last named can only divide or combine ideas acquired via the first two methods. We don't hear a great deal more about ideas of memory in *PHK* hereafter.) The sense of sight yields ideas of light and colour, the sense of touch yields ideas of hardness and softness, that of smell yields ideas of odour, etc. Where several ideas are found to occur together, we tend to think of these ideas as composing one thing and use a single name to denote it. For example, a certain array of ideas of taste, colour, shape and texture we call 'an apple', while 'Other collections of ideas *constitute* a stone, a tree, a book and the like sensible things' (emphasis added). (Note how unobtrusively Berkeley introduces the notion that all the objects we perceive are literally made of ideas. This is still of course only *PHK*'s first paragraph.)

§2 Having introduced and distinguished the objects of knowledge in §1, Berkeley proceeds in this section to describe the *subject* of knowledge, the nature of the thing which does the knowing. Besides, and distinct from, all the above-mentioned ideas, is the thing that has the ideas – that substantial thing that perceives the ideas or is otherwise aware of them. This (non-ideational) substantial something is the mind, soul or spirit. Note Berkeley always talks of minds or spirits, never of persons. As the following (slightly cryptic remark) makes clear, this is a considered usage: 'The Concrete of the Will & understanding I must call Mind not person, lest offence be given, there being but one volition acknowledged to be God. Mem: Carefully to omit Defining of Person, or making much mention of it' (*PC* 713).

The mind, soul or spirit (Berkeley uses these terms interchangeably in *PHK*) is an active thing that is able to perceive ideas or to do other operations upon them (like willing or remembering). However, the mind is not identical with any of its ideas but is rather the thing 'wherein they exist, or, which is the same thing, whereby they are perceived'. (Where ideas are perceived, there they reside.) The mind and its ideas are different and distinct things. Hence, '*Esse est percipi*' is only half the story and Berkeley's philosophy is better summarized as: '*Esse est percipi (aut percipere)*', that is, 'to be is to be perceived or to perceive'.[12] ('Percipere' includes the whole range of mental activities, obviously including perception but also the conscious, volitional activity of the will.)

Note that as early as §2 of *PHK* proper, Berkeley almost casually states that the being of perceived objects is the very same thing as their being perceived: 'for the existence of an idea consists in being perceived'. The next step is the quiet introduction of the assumptions that (1) all we can directly perceive are ideas and (2) what we directly perceive are the real things themselves. Taken all together, these premises seem to establish that we are directly acquainted with the real objects of perception but that these objects can exist only in the mind. Thus, the introduction of immaterialism is achieved with no fanfare but a fair degree of stealthy cunning. The combination of direct realism about sensible objects with the claim that such objects exist only in the mind was Berkeley's attempt at reconciling what he saw as the correct parts of both common sense and philosophy. Common sense believes we directly apprehend real things; philosophy believes the objects of our immediate experience exist only in the mind. Berkeley combined these doctrines and created thereby a kind of direct realist's idealism. Thus, Berkeley held that it is true that physical objects really are the things that we directly perceive (just as common sense maintains) and it is true that the objects of our immediate awareness really are mind-dependent entities (as philosophy maintains). Combine these doctrines and you get the real existence of directly perceived physical objects, with said real existence being entirely in the mind but nonetheless real for all that. Bear in mind that for Berkeley, the 'mental' existence and 'real' existence of sensible objects are not opposites but synonyms. Later, Berkeley will offer a criterion for distinguishing between genuine, veridical perceptions, that is, those of real sensible objects, and illusory perceptual experiences, for example, those of hallucinatory or dream objects. Just because Berkeley believed in the mind-dependence of existence, he wasn't therefore obliged to believe in the real existence of everything whose appearances the senses might present to us. As we shall see, in Berkeley's system, real objects are those whose perceptions are more vivid, continuous and steadfast, and less subject to our voluntary control, than perceptions of illusory objects.

Berkeley denies that sensible objects can possess what he later calls *absolute* existence, that is, their existing in a way which is not related to perception in any way, existence 'out of the minds of spirits, or distinct from their being perceived' (*D* 211). Indeed, Berkeley rejects not only the absolute existence of unthinking things but also the absolute existence of minds (conceived as existence distinct from perceiving or other mental activity). As Berkeley also held that physical objects are collections of sensible ideas and that collections of sensible ideas must be directly perceptible, he allows no absolute existence for physical objects either. Relative existence involves perception and is therefore possible, where absolute existence does not involve perception and is therefore impossible.[13] So, Berkeley upheld the *real* existence of *physical* things but rejected utterly the *absolute* existence of *material* things.

§3 Everybody will grant that mental objects or processes like ideas, thoughts or passions, cannot possibly exist outside the mind. Likewise, any combinations of ideas cannot exist outside of being perceived by some mind. We can acquire 'an intuitive knowledge' of this truth simply by reflecting on what the existence of sensible objects means. If I claim my table exists, I mean by this no more than that the table can be seen and felt by me. Berkeley also extends the notion of existence to include possible perception. Thus, part of what I mean when I say my table exists is that if I were placed in the right circumstances (e.g. if I were in my study) then I would see or touch the table. So, for perceived things, esse (i.e. existence or being) is percipi (i.e. being perceived). More precisely: the existence of sensible objects seemingly consists either in their being perceived or in their being perceivable: 'When, therefore, we are dealing with the perceivable, not actually being perceived by you or me, we are fully entitled to explain possible existence as possible perception. Berkeley does so, in effect, and his formula for passive existence thus expands naturally into *esse est percipi aut posse percipi*' (Luce, 1945, p. 61). Hence the 'esse' of unthinking things is not just their being perceived but also their being perceivable. Berkeley further states that it is impossible to form an idea of existence that is completely independent of any notion of perception.

Questions

1. Is Berkeley's list of the possible objects of human knowledge exhaustive?
2. Is Berkeley's initial claim (in *PHK* §1) that we can acquire ideas through attending to 'the passions and operations of the mind' in tension with his later claim that we can form no idea of the mind or its operations?
3. How convincing is the argument that physical objects are simply compounded of sensible ideas?
4. Does it follow that if all our ideas reside in the mind, any collection of ideas must also reside in the mind? Has Berkeley made a valid inference here or is he guilty of a fallacy of composition?
5. Does Berkeley argue convincingly that the ideas we perceive must reside in a substantial something that isn't an idea? Could the mind itself be simply a collection of ideas that exists without any substratum?

Unperceived existence: 'a nicer strain of abstraction' (§§4–7)

Summary

Remarkably enough, Berkeley concludes that there can be only minds (or spirits) and their ideas no later than *PHK* §7. The fundamentals of his case having been stated in *PHK* §§1–7, Berkeley then spends the rest of *PHK* exploring the consequences of his philosophy and (in particular) trying to rebut criticisms. At *PHK* 4, Berkeley does allow that we have a natural tendency to think the objects we perceive can exist somehow distinct from being present to our understanding. However, this is one apparently commonsensical opinion that will *not* survive philosophical scrutiny. This is because the 'opinion' concerned covertly nurses a contradiction within it, and so we *cannot* respect the implications of common sense metaphysics in this case, even if we tried. Sensible objects are given to us in perception and perception is necessarily of ideas.

Berkeley's attack on matter is intimately related to his attack on abstract ideas (*PHK* 5). Berkeley grants that we can conceive of certain qualities in abstraction, but only where they are capable of separate existence (cf. *PHK* Intro. 9). Thus, if I see, for example, a beach ball coloured in alternate stripes of red and blue, I can abstract from my image of this ball and consider those portions of its surface which are red, or form the idea of a beach ball which is a uniform red colour. However, I cannot abstract the redness in isolation from extension. (A 'non-extended' redness cannot be pictured or otherwise conceived.) Likewise, I can abstract from my idea of the human body and consider those parts in isolation that might be found so separated in actuality. (I can consider a head in isolation from a trunk, or a foot in isolation from a leg.)

All sensible qualities must reside in the same substance and that substance must (of course) be mental so it is impossible to consider a sensible quality existing in a state of abstraction from mental substance. Hence no sensible quality can reside in an unthinking substratum, and it's a crucial error of abstraction to think otherwise. Berkeley thought the great philosophical error was thinking the ideas of *substance* and *existence* in general can be successfully abstracted from that of specifically *mental* existent substance. Strictly speaking, all substance is, and must be, mental substance, properly understood. An unperceiving (hence non-mental) substance is a contradiction in terms. Hence material substance (defined as unperceiving) cannot exist.

Section by section
§4 For all objects that are present to the senses ('sensible objects' for short), existence is the same thing as being perceived.

Although reflection reveals *esse* is *percipi* for sensible objects, people nonetheless have a tendency to think the objects they perceive are somehow mind-independent. However, widespread though this view is, investigation reveals that it cannot possibly be correct – because it involves a contradiction. All sensible objects are simply combinations of ideas and ideas (singly or in combination) cannot exist unperceived, therefore no sensible object can exist unperceived.

§5 The oddly common belief in the mind-independent existence of sensible objects is (probably) another unfortunate consequence of the mistaken doctrine of abstract ideas. One of the great errors (perhaps the greatest error) of abstraction is thinking existence can be abstracted away from perception (or perceivability). Light, colour, heat, etc., are merely ideas and can have no existence outside the mind. Dividing ideas from their being perceived is flatly impossible – 'I might as easily divide a thing from itself'. (Berkeley seems to have logical impossibility or self-contradiction in mind – an unperceived idea, or collection of ideas, is thus a chimera on a par with a square circle.)

§6 Hence it follows (and again reflection confirms this), that all sensible objects must subsist in the mind. Furthermore, any sensible objects that stopped being perceived by me or 'any other created spirit' can be in only one of two states: either they cease to exist altogether or they exist in the mind of an eternal (i.e. non-created) spirit. The alternatives thus seem to be: either sensible objects disappear when we all close our eyes or they continue to exist through their being perceived by God. (Although §6 does not contain the word 'God', it marks the first appearance of the Deity in *PHK* proper. Clearly, the 'Eternal Spirit' Berkeley has in mind here is God. Note that while Berkeley accepts (1) that physical objects are only collections of ideas and (2) that ideas can exist only in the mind, he is not thereby committed to the intermittent existence of physical objects, or that the existence of physical objects somehow fails during gaps in finite, human perception.)

§7 Reflection reveals a further contradiction (or 'manifest repugnancy') in the notion that any kind of substance could exist *apart from* one that perceives (i.e. a mind or soul). To have an idea is to perceive that idea, or better: for an idea to exist at all is for it to be present to somebody's perception, and *thus* to reside in somebody's consciousness. Hence, ideas cannot subsist in an unperceiving, unthinking substance: 'For an idea to exist in an unperceiving thing is a manifest contradiction, for to have an idea is all one as to perceive.' In a sense, Berkeley's initial exposition of his immaterialist position is complete at this point – no later than the end of *PHK* §7. The remainder of the work can be read as attempting two tasks: (1) Berkeley's defence of immaterialism against all comers by refuting in advance as many objections to immaterialism as he can possibly think up, and (2) pointing out how desirable the consequences of immaterialism are for common sense, science, mathematics and religion. By the end, the reader should feel first, immaterialism can withstand any philosophical challenge and secondly, immaterialism is far closer to common-sense metaphysics than it initially sounds. (You may already be more of an immaterialist than you think.)

Questions

1. If existence outside the mind is truly contradictory, why do so many of us seem to believe in it? Are there other widely held beliefs that prove to be contradictory on closer examination?
2. Is the 'manifest repugnance' Berkeley finds in the concept of material (unperceivable) existence really the same as logical contradiction? If not, what sort of 'repugnance' is it?
3. In his later *D*, Berkeley laid much less emphasis on attacking abstract ideas. How close a connection is there between the belief in unperceived existence and the doctrine of abstract ideas?
4. Has a complete case for immaterialism been made by the end of *PHK* §7?
5. The title of *PHK* foregrounds human knowledge as Berkeley's subject but are his aims in (at least these early sections of) *PHK* primarily metaphysical or epistemological ones?

Problems for materialism (§§8–17)

Summary

Only ideas can resemble other ideas. Therefore, the ideas we perceive cannot resemble (or represent) any imperceptible substratum. There can be no resemblance between ideas and anything imperceptible. (We certainly can't have acquired the concept of unperceived existence from perceiving any existent in an unperceived state.)

Berkeley rejects Locke's doctrine that we could be ignorant of the nature of a directly perceptible quality like colour. Furthermore, he rejects both 'subjectivity' and 'resemblance' criteria for distinguishing primary from secondary qualities. *Contra* the subjectivity criterion, he maintains all the arguments materialists have used to prove that secondary qualities reside in the mind actually show that the so-called primary qualities are subjective too. Using his account of abstraction, Berkeley argues thus: consider any visual expanse – you cannot frame in your imagination any visual extension that is completely colourless. (To be clear: imagining a transparent pane of glass or a whirling body of point gas-molecules is *not* picturing a colourless visual expanse.) Likewise, you cannot visualize a coloured expanse without giving it *some* sort of shape, and thus some sort of extension too. Any alleged visual object that completely lacked extension or shape would be impossible to visualize and so wouldn't truly be a *visual* object at all. So, Berkeley argues, if we cannot conceive of a visual object that possesses extension without colour and we cannot conceive of a visual object that possesses colour without also possessing extension, colour and extension (supposedly secondary and primary qualities respectively) are inextricably intertwined. What cannot be conceived to exist in isolation cannot so exist in fact, therefore wherever colour ultimately resides, so then must extension, and vice versa.

Contra the resemblance criterion, Berkeley argues that no perceptible thing (like a visual idea of extension or of colour) can possibly resemble (and hence represent) an imperceptible thing. Any imperceptible causes that secondary qualities might have obviously cannot be given to us through perception. Any relations between perceptible and imperceptible objects cannot be apprehended through the senses. Berkeley adheres to a 'Likeness Principle' for representation, whereby there can be no representation without resemblance between the represented and that which does the representing. Furthermore, there can be no resemblance without (at least possible) presentation to consciousness. (Cf. 'Two things cannot be said to be alike or unlike till they have been compar'd', *PC* 378.) So (Berkeley claims) where one of the objects to be compared cannot be presented to consciousness, talk of resemblance between them is meaningless. We cannot know how (or to what extent) our sensible ideas resemble their supposed imperceptible, external, material causes. For Berkeley, all qualities (be they supposedly primary or secondary) reside in the mind, and it's meaningless to talk of our sensible ideas somehow resembling or copying imperceptible, mind-independent archetypes.

Although the correct construal of Berkeley's views on the impossibility of material substance remains controversial, he clearly did not think that material substance does exist or *just happens* not to exist.[14] There are many imaginable objects which don't exist but which could have – *contingent* non-existents. Consider unicorns: even if biology forbids unicorns, logic offers no reason why a horse-like animal couldn't grow an ornate horn, like a narwhal's tusk, out of its forehead. So unicorns seem merely *contingently* non-existent; although none actually exist, they could have. Contrast the contingently non-existent unicorn with the *necessarily* non-existent square circle. A circle is a plane figure whose entire circumference is equidistant from a single point. A square is a four-sided equiangular plane figure. One and the same figure cannot simultaneously be square and circular. If Berkeley is correct, matter (or perception-independent substance) is not contingently non-existent (like unicorns), but necessarily non-existent (like square circles). If Berkeley is right, every existent must be related to perception (actual or possible) and hence materialism is conceptually impossible.

The chief problems Berkeley poses for materialism are:

- The notion of matter is incoherent. Qualities like extension (*et al.*) must exist only as ideas in the mind. If ideas can only be like other ideas, neither they nor their patterns (or archetypes) can exist in any non-mental substance (*PHK* 9). Our ideas of sense cannot be caused by, or even take their pattern from, any kind of imperceptible, unthinking substance.
- Materialism leads to indirect realism about perception, and thence to scepticism. Although ideas cannot have a mind-independent existence, they are supposed by materialists to

copy mind-independent existents (*PHK* 15). But the objects of sense continually vary and yet their originals are supposed to be unchanging, so they can't truly copy their originals (ibid.).

- The notion of matter is empty (*PHK* 17). The only idea we can possibly entertain of matter is that of bare undifferentiated existence. However, even this thin conception of material substance is unsustainably vague and abstract.

Section by section
§8 Berkeley then considers an objection: granted that ideas cannot exist outwith the mind, could they not still *copy* extra-mental material objects? (This is essentially the view of a materialist representationalist about perception.) Berkeley replies that this misconstrues (and greatly overstates) the capacity that ideas have to resemble or to represent things. Again, reflection reveals that ideas cannot resemble or represent anything but other ideas. (Hence Berkeley accepts a 'Likeness Principle': representation must involve likeness and presentation to consciousness.) We can't conceive a likeness between any perceived idea and any non-perceivable thing: '. . . We shall find it impossible for us to conceive a likeness except only between our ideas'. If we are asked to imagine that ideas represent 'those supposed originals or external things' entertained by materialists, there are only two possibilities: either the alleged external objects are perceivable or they aren't. If they are perceivable, then they themselves are ideas. If however these objects aren't perceivable, then ideas cannot resemble them and so cannot represent them either. (Berkeley appeals to the reader to decide whether or not a colour can be like something invisible or a texture like something impalpable, etc.)

§9 We now turn to another key Lockean doctrine (although not one original to Locke): the primary–secondary qualities distinction. Candidates for primary qualities might include: extension, solidity, shape, motion, etc. Candidates for secondary qualities might include: colour, shading, texture, sound, etc. There have been various attempts at distinguishing between the two kinds of quality. One significant criterion (a.k.a. 'the resemblance criterion') held that secondary qualities are not supposed to resemble, or to be directly copied from, external properties, whereas primary qualities are supposed to resemble their external originals. (Another way to distinguish primary from secondary qualities is to say that the latter depend for their existence on being perceived, or present to a percipient, whereas the latter are not observer-dependent.) These putative external properties are supposed to reside in a substance called *matter*, which is supposed to be an extended but inert substratum that neither perceives nor is perceptible, but somehow supports or causes those qualities that we do perceive. However, drawing on his previous conclusions about where ideas must reside, Berkeley argues that extension, motion and shape have already been shown to reside in the mind, and to do so of necessity, that is, such qualities cannot reside anywhere else but in the mind. Furthermore, given that only ideas can resemble ideas, it follows that nothing like an idea can reside in matter either. So ideas cannot be patterned after, or have archetypes that reside in, matter. (Cf. 'no idea *or archetype of an idea* can exist otherwise than in a mind', *D* 212–13, emphasis added.) Properly understood, the very idea of matter (or 'corporeal substance') is contradictory, that is, it involves postulating that qualities that can only reside in mental substance can somehow reside in a non-mental substance.

§10 Further to the primary/secondary qualities distinction, there is another way of distinguishing them (a.k.a. 'the subjectivity criterion'). Many of those who believe that primary qualities exist in a corporeal (i.e. unthinking) substance also assert that secondary qualities reside in the mind, and that secondary qualities somehow depend on the purely corporeal qualities of matter. Berkeley claims that such separability of the primary and secondary qualities (e.g. such that one resides in material substance and the other in mental substance) will not do. The so-called primary and secondary qualities are inextricably intermingled and where the one resides, so then must the other.

Berkeley is here almost certainly indebted to Pierre Bayle (1647–1706), particularly the 'Zeno of Elea' entry in Bayle's *Dictionary*.[15] Bayle attributes this argument to Simon Foucher's (1644–96) 1675 critique of Malebranche's *Recherche*.[16] Foucher accused Malebranche of offering no reasons why extension and solidity could not reside in the mind, just as colour and odour are supposed to. If objects can merely *appear* to be coloured to our perception without being so, perhaps they can also appear to be extended without being so. Colour and (visual) extension are not readily separable.

Again Berkeley challenges the reader to picture qualities like motion and extension existing in isolation from all other qualities. Primary qualities cannot be conceived to exist in such isolation. (Visual extension cannot be imagined without colour, nor can colour be imagined to exist separately from visual extension.) Since ideas of colour must reside in the mind, and primary and secondary qualities cannot reside in separate substances, it follows then that the alleged primary qualities can only exist in the mind likewise.

§11 Furthermore, everyone acknowledges that comparative or relational qualities (e.g. relative sizes or motions) are dependent upon the position and movement of the perceiver. ('Big' and 'small', 'fast' and 'slow' seem inescapably observer-dependent.) Hence Berkeley concludes (perhaps too swiftly) that any extension (or motion) that existed outside the mind would have to be somehow distinct from all these relative determinations. Therefore, any mind-independent extension (motion) would have to be neither big nor small (fast nor slow), and hence would be no extension (motion) at all. So, Berkeley reasons, if motion or extension are determinables which have to exist in one determinate form, and all determinate forms are mind-dependent then so too must extension and motion be. (An extension that isn't a particular, determinate extension is something Berkeley holds to be impossible. Likewise a motion that isn't fast, slow or somewhere in between the two is no motion.)

Should anyone attempt to dispute this last claim by retorting that the external extension is somehow 'extension in general', then Berkeley retorts, this ploy merely illustrates the kinship between the doctrine of material substance and the doctrine of abstract general ideas. Finally, if solidity requires extension and extension is demonstrably capable of existing only in the mind then solidity too can exist only in the mind. So whatever 'real' material objects might be like, they can't even be held to be extended or to possess a shape. However, one problem with the argument of this section is that Berkeley seems to move too quickly from perceptual relativity to mind-dependence to mind-only existence. That objects seem to possess different properties from different perspectives or to different percipients does not *prove* that one of these properties can't genuinely reside in the object.

§12 Berkeley continues: number too is inescapably mind-dependent (even to those who believe in the external existence of other qualities and properties) and numerical properties vary according to acts of the mind. For example, there is nothing intrinsic to a length of, for example, 1 yard which forces us to consider it as 1 length, 3 lengths (i.e. 3 feet) or 36 lengths (i.e. 36 inches). Only an arbitrary act of the mind determines which numbers are attached to which qualities (or combinations of ideas). As above, Berkeley again seems to take it as established that mind-dependence must equal mind-only existence and it's not clear that this identification is compelling. (As we shall notice again below, Berkeley's particularism goes too far in making relations and resemblances mind-dependent as well as numbers.)

§13 There is no plausible candidate for an idea that accompanies all our perceptions. Unity is sometimes alleged to be a simple idea that somehow accompanies all other ideas but this is simply false. Introspection does not reveal any such ubiquitous idea and we can be confident in this result, because if the idea of unity were an inevitable accompaniment of all our other ideas, then unity should be the most familiar (and oft-presented) idea of all.

§14 Berkeley continues: the arguments that materialists use to prove the mind-dependence of the secondary qualities can be equally well deployed to establish that the primary qualities are mind-dependent too. For example, heat and cold are held to be mind-dependent ('affections only of the mind, and not at all patterns of real beings') – no one with any grasp of the relativity of perception would think that heat as we feel it literally resides in hot coals. There are several familiar arguments to this effect. Consider one of the best-known examples of perceptual relativity: if you place one hand in a bucket full of ice and the other hand in a hot bath, then place both hands in a tepid bowl of water, the water in the bowl will feel hot to the hand lately in the ice but cold to the hand just withdrawn from the hot bath. Unless we are to attribute contradictory properties to the bowlful of water, the properties heat and cold as we perceive them cannot reside in the water in the bowl and seem necessarily to reside in the perceiver. However while this result is familiar enough, Berkeley says that exactly parallel arguments can be made about supposedly primary qualities like extension or number. The same extension will present different appearances to the same percipient at different locations or to different percipients at the same location. Just as illness can change sweet tastes to bitter by affecting the palate, so can apparent motion speed up or slow down accordingly as the succession of ideas in the percipient's mind speeds up or slows down. If tastes or feelings of heat are to be placed in the mind on grounds of observer-relativity, then so too should motion, extension, shape and the rest of the supposed primary qualities.

Admittedly, Berkeley doesn't always observe the subtleties of Locke's account of the primary/secondary distinction. For example, Lockean secondary qualities can be defined as those configurations of primaries that produce (sensory) ideas in human percipients: 'when such configurations [of primary qualities] are characterized as powers to produce ideas in us, then they are called "secondary qualities"'.[17] This notion of secondaries as idea-causing configurations of primaries isn't expressly discussed by Berkeley. Likewise, Berkeley doesn't address Locke's account of *tertiary qualities*, that is, those arrangements of ideas which have the power to cause ideas *in other substances*:

> The Sun has a *power* to blanch Wax, and Wax a *power* to be blanched by the Sun, whereby the Yellowness is destroy'd, and the Whiteness made to exist in its room. In which, and the like cases, the *Power* we consider is in reference to the change of perceivable *Ideas*. (*Essay* II/xxi/1)

In all these cases, Berkeley would presumably reiterate that no intelligible model of causation can attribute casual efficacy to imperceptible objects or qualities. Had Berkeley considered Locke's tertiary qualities, presumably he would have argued that, while changes in the (sensible) ideas answering to different physical objects would be observable, Locke would still have to refer such changes to some concatenation of powers residing (imperceptibly) in the objects themselves. Hence, while

Berkeley didn't explicitly consider tertiary qualities, it seems such qualities wouldn't have posed any special problems for his objections to Locke and materialist representationalism generally.

§15 So, Berkeley concludes, materialist arguments that primary and secondary qualities differ because the former are outwith the mind and the latter are mind-dependent fail. However, Berkeley also notes that this argument will only take his immaterialism so far – the materialist's failure to establish the mind-independence of primary qualities may only establish the weaker conclusion that we know nothing of what the true causes of our ideas are like and not the stronger conclusion that all existence must be in the mind. As Berkeley makes quite clear, while the weak conclusion is a useful stepping-stone for him, it's really the latter, stronger conclusion that his purposes require. However, Berkeley is not without resources for bootstrapping his way from the weak conclusion to the stronger one. For example, he can appeal to his earlier arguments that no quality like colour or taste can exist independently of the mind. So where the perceptual relativity of primary qualities does not prove mind-dependence alone, it may become decisive if combined with the mind-dependence of secondary qualities *and* the co-location of primary and secondary qualities.

§16 Where materialists often invoke matter as a substance (or substratum) that supports modes (or qualities) like extension, Berkley thinks we have no positive idea of matter. The materialist might reply that although lacking a *positive* idea of matter (i.e. an enumeration of its intrinsic qualities or how it is in itself), we can form a *relative* idea of it (i.e. an enumeration of how matter appears to us or how it stands in relation to other objects). Thus, the materialist might say, we may not be able to picture the qualities that matter possesses but we might still be able to grasp the relations it stands in to other things that we can perceive. Berkeley challenges the materialist to explain what relation can exist between matter and the qualities it supposedly supports. (We cannot perceive relations of support between perceptible qualities and imperceptible substratum.) What sort of support can this be? Clearly, a literal construal of 'support' won't do – matter cannot support qualities like extension or solidity in the way that a pillar supports a building. But if the literal construal is impossible, what other kind is there in this case?

§17 Berkeley further maintains that if we look closely at the supposed idea of matter or material substance, all we can find is the mere idea of existence joined with the (unspecified) idea of the supporting of qualities, that is, the alleged idea of matter is reduced a mere 'empty notion', that of 'Being in general, together with the relative notion of its supporting accidents'. Of all ideas, being is 'the most abstract and incomprehensible'. The notion of existence *in general* (i.e. without any reference to perception or to differentiating or particular qualities) seems the most abstract (and hence unclear) notion possible and the notion of support involved is similarly unclear. (So matter is an unsustainable idea of support joined to an unsustainable idea of existence.) But really even this much analysis is unnecessary – Berkeley takes it as having been previously established that no existent can possibly be outwith the mind and so material substance is necessarily ruled out.

Questions

1. Even if we grant Berkeley that primary and secondary qualities cannot be conceived in isolation from each other, must we therefore accept their inseparability in actuality?
2. Besides the 'subjectivity' and 'resemblance' criteria for distinguishing primary and secondary qualities, could this distinction be drawn in other ways? If so, could these alternative criteria escape some of Berkeley's strictures?
3. Does the appeal to perceptual relativity succeed in establishing the mind-dependence of all qualities? Is there a distinction to be drawn between mind-relative existence and mind-dependent existence?
4. Even in the face of the above arguments, can we frame a more positive conception of matter than simply that of 'Being in general'?

A Cartesian 'dream' argument (§§18–21)

Summary

As part of his arguments for rationalism, Descartes offered his 'dream' and 'evil demon' arguments for distrusting the senses. Dreams can contain all manner of experiences that seem convincing, but which vanish utterly on waking and need have no connection with real events. Likewise, it's conceivable that an evil external power is permanently controlling all our senses and feeding us a systematically false perceptual world. Both arguments suggest that all our senses could be radically and permanently mistaken. Hence, Descartes concluded, certainty cannot be derived from the unregulated senses, and we need to use reason to determine that such hypotheses are unsustainable (i.e. because God has furnished us with a power to discriminate between trustworthy and untrustworthy ideas).

While rejecting Cartesian distrust of the senses, Berkeley did exploit Descartes' 'dream' argument in attacking material substance. Berkeley took up the view held by Descartes (and others) that veridical and hallucinatory experiences can have the same perceptual content. In particular, he adopted the premise that perception cannot reveal whether our experiences have external or internal causes. Berkeley argues thus: it is universally acknowledged that all our sensory appearances might have been exactly the same even if no material substance had existed. If so, all the sensory appearances materialists invoke to prove the existence of matter could be exactly as they are even if matter did not exist. Why then should we infer that any such thing exists? It seems that everyone (even materialists) agrees that we can dream up seeming existents that aren't there. If all the sensible appearances invoked to prove the existence of matter could be as they are without any such substratum existing then matter seems explanatorily redundant.

Berkeley next imagines the materialist arguing that we might at least be able to assume that our ideas *probably* resemble, and may be caused by, material bodies. At this point, Berkeley deploys the problem of mind/body interaction against materialism, that is, the problem of how mental events can causally interact with physical events. Nobody, least of all the monist materialist, seems able to explain how material objects might cause ideas of perception. A causal link from physical to mental is not even intelligible. It's beyond anyone's comprehension how an extended substance might produce sensible ideas, hence no materialist can explain how matter can cause sensible ideas or how ideas can have physical effects. We cannot picture any such process or even vaguely guess at how such a link might function. However, we do have an intelligible model of mental causation – our own experience reveals that mental events can be causally linked to other mental events. (If we decide to entertain a certain idea, or train of ideas, then those ideas duly appear at our behest.) Our minds are not simply bundles of ideas but agents; self-conscious and self-motivating beings who can understand our own purposes and will our own actions. Through agency, mental causation is familiar to us, where material causation is utterly mysterious. Idealism has no problem of mind/body interaction – if there is only one substance, there can be no *inter*action. Granted, monistic materialism faces no interaction problem either but Berkeley holds that only idealism affords a truly comprehensible model of causality.

Section by section

§18 Supposing though that we grant at least the bare possibility of matter and that this matter somehow corresponds to some of our ideas. Berkeley then asks how we could possibly know that such a thing existed. Two possibilities suggest themselves: 'Either we must know it by sense, or by reason.' However, neither will work. The senses can only bring us into contact with ideas but (as materialists acknowledge) cannot inform us of the existence of anything imperceptible or that lies outside the mind. Maybe then we grasp matter through reason, inferring that something exists behind the ideas we perceive. But reason cannot reveal the existence of matter either. The problem is that nobody believes that there is a necessary connection between our ideas and what causes them. Even ordinary perceptual situations are full of possibilities for error. In more extreme cases (such as illness, dreaming or hallucination), we can be presented with a panoply of non-existent objects that don't remotely resemble their causes. Indeed, it's accepted by everyone that all our perceptual experiences might be exactly the same (in terms of content) even if there were no external objects causing them at all. (Here Berkeley is drawing on something like the oft-assumed and almost universally granted coherence of Descartes' 'evil demon' hypothesis.) So we don't need to believe in external bodies as the causes of our ideas, since at least some of the time (and conceivably all of the time) we can have ideas that bear no resemblance or relationship to external bodies.

There is no necessity that our ideas have to have an absolutely existing external (material) cause, since any idea that can be attributed to the causal efficacy of material substance could be generated without any such substance being in existence. So even if we were to grant to materialists (which Berkeley most certainly doesn't grant) that matter was a coherent possibility and so might at least be able to exist, it would still be the case that matter was explanatorily useless. So, in a nutshell, matter cannot exist and even if it could exist, we could have no reason to believe in its existence.

However, this last argument of Berkeley's can be challenged. For all that Berkeley resisted materialist representationalism (i.e. that our ideas are caused by and represent an imperceptible substratum), seemingly he did not abandon representationalism *per se*. According to one form of representationalism (called *intentionalism*), 'perceptual experience is a type of mental representation, where the phenomenal character of a given perceptual experience is determined by the content of the representation (rather than the world itself)'.[18] In other words, intentionalism holds that two experiences can have quite distinct causes but identical phenomenal content (or phenomenal contents that are at least indistinguishable from the perceiver's perspective). This last premise also involves what M. G. F. Martin has called the 'common kind assumption', that is, that 'perceptual experiences form a common kind of mental state among cases of veridical perception, illusion and hallucination'.[19]

The 'common kind assumption' rests on epistemological premises that many philosophers now regard as controversial or at least non-obvious. Contrast the above intentional view with that known as disjunctivism:

> A theory is disjunctive insofar as it distinguishes genuine from non-genuine cases of some phenomenon P on the grounds that no salient feature of cases of one type is common to cases of the other type. Genuine and non-genuine cases of P are, in this sense, fundamentally different. (Blatti, 2006, p. 856)

The argument from 'dream' scepticism (or perceptual illusion) is often used as Berkeley uses it, that is, to suggest that when we are having illusory/hallucinatory experience, we cannot tell whether or not our experience is of a mind-independent object. However, the disjunctivist concludes, this doesn't mean that we are not (and never can be) aware of mind-independent objects. It means something less dramatic instead, that is, that we do not experience mind-independent objects when we are hallucinating, dreaming or otherwise subject to perceptual illusions. Disjunctivism gets its name because it claims that the correct report of, for example, a visual experience of a tree would be 'Either I am actually seeing a tree or I am having an illusory experience which is indistinguishable from that of seeing a tree' (see Blatti, 2006, p. 856). So, for the disjunctivist, the experience is not characterized solely by its representational content. Whither, I hear you cry, has Berkeley gone to in this digression in the philosophy of perception? Well, Berkeley seems to accept the common kind assumption and uses it as a crucial part of his arguments against material substance. However, as the possibility of a disjunctivist account of perception shows, we need not make the assumption (which to be fair was more or less unquestioned in Berkeley's day) that phenomenal content determines representation. (Also, the Likeness Principle suggests Berkeley would be hard pressed to relax his adherence to the common kind assumption.)

§19 Anyway, with the above excursus about common kinds set to one side, we come to the next step in Berkeley's argument against matter. As Berkeley recognizes, the materialist is unlikely to give up just yet. Berkeley then imagines the materialist retreating to explanatory ease and probability. Thus, the materialist might argue that the job of explaining our sensations is at least facilitated by postulating some external substance, and that surely it is at least more probable than not that bodies exist outside our minds. Here Berkeley invokes the problem of mind/body interaction. (This problem arises for dualists like Descartes, who believe that certain events in the necessarily extended realm of space somehow can both cause, and be caused by, events in the utterly non-spatial realm of the mind.) If indeed our ideas are caused by a material substance which is extended, inert and qualitatively entirely unlike our ideas of sense, how then can material properties cause the generation of ideas? By what mechanism can two such unlike substances possibly be joined? We simply have no conception at all of how 'body can act upon spirit' (or vice versa), and we cannot form any such conception either. Thus, the generation of our ideas would remain 'equally inexplicable' whether or not we believe in the existence of matter. So, even if once again we grant (purely for the sake of argument) that matter is a coherent and possible existent, there is no explanatory advantage in so doing. Indeed, there's even a sort of theological 'Ockham's razor'[20] problem here (at least for theistic materialists – among whom Berkeley would number Descartes and Malebranche), namely the problem of why God would elect to bring into existence many examples of a substance that seems completely redundant. Anyone who chooses to believe in matter does so on shaky grounds and can't expect that this belief should be found at all compelling. (Although Berkeley doesn't say so in so many words, he seems here to be charging the materialist with a kind of *fideism* about matter, that is, embracing a belief in matter not through a process of reasoning and attending to probability but through faith. One difference of course between material-ist fideism and theistic fideism is that Berkeley would regard the inference to God as one which leads to a coherent and use-ful hypothesis, whereas any inference to matter would lead to an obscure, incoherent and unhelpful hypothesis. Berkeley of course held that the existence of God was capable of rational demonstration.)

§20 Effectively summarizing the preceding two sections and pursuing the 'Cartesian' argument about dreams and hallucin-ations, Berkeley argues that if there were external bodies, we couldn't possibly know that they existed (i.e. they couldn't yield ideas of themselves that can be presented to consciousness). Furthermore, if such bodies *didn't* exist, then we wouldn't know that either – our experiences might be exactly the same whether or not any such things as material bodies existed. Where then is the added explanatory value in burdening our philosophical systems and inflating our ontology with an entity so apparently useless? (Again, although Berkeley doesn't invoke Ockham or his famous principle of ontological economy here, his argument is thoroughly Ockhamist in spirit.) Berkeley offers a hypothet-ical example to strengthen this point: we can surely imagine that 'an intelligence' could have precisely the same experiences that we have (including all of those experiences which are supposed to support the inference to material substance) even if no external bodies whatever existed. Such an intelligence would be (by hypothesis) in just the same evidential position as we are in with respect to the existence of matter, yet surely it would be a mistake for this intelligence to embrace materialism. (The moral is: what would be a mistaken inference for the intelligence would also be a mistaken inference for any being that was in exactly the intelligence's evidential position, for example, beings like us. If Berkeley's hypothetical 'intelligence' would be mistaken in embracing even the probable truth of materialism on the strength of such uncompelling evidence then so would 'any reasonable person' and hence so should we.)

§21 Besides encouraging philosophical errors and profitless disputes, materialism is also highly conducive to the generation of theological errors (and 'impieties') too. However, Berkeley declines to expatiate further on these disadvantages here, partly because he returns to theological difficulties for the materialist (at *PHK* §§85–96) but also because he thinks that demonstrating *a priori* the logical impossibility of matter trumps any *a posteriori* appeal to disadvantages in materialism and makes any further objections redundant. (It's one thing to show that your opponent's doctrine is merely inconvenient, it's another thing to show that it's factually mistaken; and quite a third thing to convict your opponent of self-contradiction or logical error – presumably the latter is absolutely fatal.) If material substance is demonstrably incoherent, then the case against matter is hardly strengthened by pointing out that belief in matter has undesirable or implausible consequences. However, Berkeley tries to bolster his case even for those who don't accept his *a priori* demolition of the concept of matter by emphasizing that matter would still be an uncompelling postulate even if it existed.

Questions
1. Assuming that radical sceptical hypotheses are coherent, does this render matter a redundant postulate?
2. Is the idealist in a better position than the dualist when it comes to making causation between our volitions and our bodies intelligible?

3. Even if Berkeley's 'intelligence' (who receives false appearances of matter) would be wrong to believe in matter, does the same hold true for us?

The 'Master Argument' (§§22–4)

Summary

Gamely, Berkeley now stakes the success of his immaterialism, and his entire philosophical project, on an appeal to the reader's imaginative faculties. He challenges his readers to imagine the possibility of anything existing other than in a mind. Perhaps needless to say, Berkeley feels he can afford this concession, because he is challenging his opponent to a gamble he can't lose and the materialist can't win. Berkeley thinks he can only be defeated on this point by someone who can entertain a contradictory object of thought, namely someone who can conceive of an object without conceiving of it. However, this argument is open to numerous challenges and has duly been much challenged.

Section by section

§22 The apparent logical triumph of immaterialism now seems to give Berkeley cause for pause, and he reflects that perhaps his demonstration has been 'needlessly prolix' when materialism can really be demolished much more swiftly. Indeed, an appeal to mere introspection should do the job: examine your ideas of, for example, sound, colour, motion and then try to imagine them existing without presentation to consciousness. It can't be done and your attempt must fail, but at least making the attempt should help convince you that you were attempting to pull off a contradictory feat. Thus, to hypothetical conceivers of unconceived objects, Berkeley says:

> I am content to put the whole upon this issue; if you can but conceive it possible for one extended moveable substance, or in general, for any one idea or any thing like an idea, to exist otherwise than in a mind perceiving it, I shall readily give up the cause . . . [T]he bare possibility of your opinion's being true, shall pass for an argument that it is so.

Although not explicitly stated here, at least two vital premises for this argument need to be spelled out. The first of these premises is a conceivability account of possibility, that is, that what we can conceive of sets the boundaries of what is actually possible. (The second premise we will hear more about below, since it concerns the relation between perception and conception, which Berkeley discusses in §23.) Berkeley gave perhaps his clearest statement of a conceivability criterion of possibility, one which links existence, conceivability and abstraction, in his draft introduction to *PHK*:

It is, I think, a receiv'd axiom that an impossibility cannot be conceiv'd. For what created intelligence will pretend to conceive, that which God cannot cause to be? Now it is on all hands agreed, that nothing abstract or general can be made really to exist, whence it should seem to follow, that it cannot have so much as an ideal existence in the understanding. (*Works*, Luce-Jessop edition, vol. II, p. 125)

It also seems to have long been a settled belief of Berkeley's that to imagine something is precisely to imagine it as existing. (Cf. *PC* 792: 'The Existence of anything imaginable is nothing different from imagination or perception.') Indeed, he seems to have held that existence can be indifferently allowed to the objects of perception or imagination (with the caveat that purely imaginary objects present a less vivid, stable and coherent set of appearances). In other words, Berkeley framing an idea of something in the mind establishes that the thing conceived of is at least a possible existent. However, Berkeley needs a stronger premise than this, namely that our being unable to conceive of something establishes that it is not a possible existent. Berkeley needs to establish not just that conceivability implies possibility, but that inconceivability implies impossibility. Why should we allow Berkeley this assumption? Conceivability, perceivability and logical possibility are simply not the same thing – worse still, none of the three subsumes any of the others (save for the caveat that presumably anything perceivable must be logically possible). For example, I can't visualize a four-dimensional space-time geometry but (I'm told) I live in one, *ergo* space-time must be a possible existent. Then again, I can (in some sense) conceive that Gödel's theorems might have proved false but (again I'm told) such is logically impossible.

§23 Further to the challenge issued in §22, Berkeley considers (and tries to defuse) an objection while continuing his appeal to the reader's powers of imagination:

> But say you, surely there is nothing easier than to imagine trees, for instance, in a park, or books existing in a closet, and no body by to perceive them. I answer, you may so, there is no difficulty in it: but what is all this, I beseech you, more than framing in your mind certain ideas which you call *books* and *trees*, and at the same time omitting to frame the idea of any one that may perceive them? But do not you your self perceive or think of them all the while? This therefore is nothing to the purpose: it only shows you have the power of imagining or forming ideas in your mind; but it doth not shew that you can conceive it possible, the objects of your thought may exist without the mind: to make out this, it is necessary that you conceive them existing unconceived or unthought of, which is a manifest repugnancy. When we do our utmost to conceive the existence of external bodies, we are all the while only contemplating our own ideas. But the mind taking no notice of itself, is deluded to think it can and doth conceive bodies existing unthought of or without the mind; though at the same time they are apprehended by or exist in itself.

While Gallois (1974) dubbed this the 'Master Argument', few commentators or critics have felt themselves mastered by it.[21] (A similar argument appears at *D* 200–1) The name 'Master Argument' is apt more because Berkeley thinks this argument decisive and is prepared to stake his entire project on its success, than because it has bested all comers.

On the face of it, Berkeley has simply been guilty of a rather obvious (and even rather grotesque) fallacy here. (David Stove even dubbed a version of this argument 'The Worst Argument in the World', although not so much to batter Berkeley as to undermine what he saw as unreflective scepticism.)[22] Perhaps Berkeley has inadmissibly conflated perception and conception, but then Berkeley would maintain that this conflation is itself necessary. Another way to express the 'conflation' objection: Berkeley conflates the *representation* (the idea presented to consciousness) with the *represented* (the thing the representation depicts). The classic statement of this objection is due to George Pitcher: 'The distinction, couched in terms of ideas, is between what an idea is an idea *of*, and the idea itself; couched in terms of representation, it is the distinction between what is represent*ed*, and what represents'.[23] Thus, one might object, just because we cannot conceive of something without in some sense representing it to ourselves, it does not follow that the object concerned cannot exist without thus being represented.

As Jonathan Dancy puts it (1998, introduction to *PHK*, p. 27), it sounds as if the Master Argument falls down because the analogy between conceiving the unconceived and seeing the unseen is flawed: 'It is true that I cannot conceive of something while nobody is conceiving of it. But I can conceive of things *as* having properties that (as I am well aware) they have not got.' Of my currently 5-feet-tall-friend Jane, I can truly imagine that she might have been 6 feet tall. This is of course distinct from imagining Jane as being *simultaneously* 5 feet tall and 6 feet tall, which would be contradictory. However, Berkeley would reply: granted you can visualize Jane as she would appear had she been 6 feet tall, you cannot visualize Jane as she would appear if she had been imperceptible. (In any event, as we shall, Berkeley thinks that appealing to counterfactual perceptual situations is still to make perception the key to existence – see below on §§46–8 and phenomenalism.)

Why then does Berkeley place such confidence in the 'Master Argument'? Partly, as the 'books in the closet' example suggests, Berkeley thought that any belief in the continued existence of objects outwith their being perceived is in some way self-fulfilling. Once an object has been conceived of, its status as a (possible) object of perception is guaranteed. However, Mackie (1976) claims that Berkeley's 'books in the closet' example mistakes an operational self-refutation with a true self-contradiction: the conception of something existing unconceived is operationally self-refuting but not self-contradictory.[24] (Consider the way that a person uttering in a loud voice the sentence 'I am silent' would operationally refute itself. Uttering such a sentence aloud is in some sense self-defeating although the proposition expressed in the sentence is not actually self-contradictory.)

Given its apparent centrality to Berkeley's project, what can (if anything) be done to rescue the Master Argument? On a more generous interpretation of the Master Argument (upheld by, for example, Winkler, 1989, pp. 184–7), Berkeley is attacking the very conceivability of the unperceived existence of physical (hence sensible) bodies. In trying to conceive of existent bodies outwith our minds, 'we are all the while only contemplating our own ideas'. This kind of conception is far from proving the possibility that objects can genuinely exist in the absence of conception. In trying to conceive of existent bodies outwith our minds, we are still only picturing to ourselves a series of ideas but ones which we don't explicitly refer to perception. The possibility of this kind of conception is far from proving that objects can genuinely exist in the complete absence of conception. As noted above, Berkeley often relies (implicitly or explicitly) on some form of conceivability criterion of possibility, that is, what cannot be represented to the mind cannot be conceived and what cannot be conceived cannot exist. This then suggests a two-stage Master Argument:

> *Stage 1: We cannot represent to ourselves a non-perceived existence because such an existence cannot be a possible object of perception.*
> *Stage 2: What cannot be represented to the mind cannot be conceived and what cannot be conceived cannot exist.*
> *Hence: No unperceived existence is possible.*

This reconstruction of the Master Argument has at least two advantages: first, it does mesh with Berkeley's conceivability criterion of possibility, and secondly, it might be bolstered by appeal to Berkeley's 'Divine Language' view of nature (cf. *PHK* §§148–9). If God created the natural world and its constituent ideas of sense as part of a language, any entity that could not possibly be presented to the senses has no sufficient reason to exist. (Just as an imperceptible letter or word could have no function or place in a human language.) Thus, if we accept the Divine Language model of nature, we might allow Berkeley that ontology recapitulates epistemology, that is, that the furniture of the world was designed with our convenience in mind and therefore what we cannot imagine has no place in existence.

On this interpretation, the combination of Berkeley's Master Argument and Divine Language model of Nature produce results that have something in common with the 'Principle of Sufficient Reason' (PSR), upheld by Gottfried Wilhelm Leibniz (1646–1716). The PSR holds that 'Nothing happens without a sufficient reason why it should be thus rather than otherwise'.[25] The PSR is effectively a test of whether or nor a putative entity can exist.[26] Although Leibniz and Berkeley both (in different ways) upheld the mind-dependence of existence, Leibniz arrived at a version of idealism on strictly rationalist principles. Both Leibniz and Berkeley seemingly held that the existence and properties of objects must be capable of analysis as results of the rational deliberations of an agent creator. However, Leibniz's PSR denies any arbitrariness in God's way with Creation, whereas Berkeley insists that the laws of nature and the sensible ideas they relate could have been installed differently, if God had so wished. Cf. Leibniz: 'All in all that method of creating a world is chosen which involves more reality or perfection, and God acts like the greatest geometer, who prefers the best constructions of problems'.[27]

However, as Lisa Downing points out, even the more generous two-stage version of the Master Argument is itself open to challenge, not least because it presupposes a '*representationalist theory of perception*'.[28] Thus, what we can perceive is restricted by the scope of what can be represented to us. The Master Argument then runs roughly thus: we cannot represent lack of conception or lack of perception to ourselves via ideas that embody (or resemble) these properties (on pain of self-contradiction), *ergo* we cannot perceive or conceptualize unperceived or unconceptualized existence. Thus, part of the blame for the failure of the Master Argument might lie with Berkeley's not fully freeing himself from the representationalism he attacked in Malebranche and Locke.[29] Berkeley may have emancipated himself from representational *materialism* but without giving up representationalism as such.[30]

Further to defending, or at least ameliorating the Master Argument: there are at least three reasons why Berkeley might have made himself particularly susceptible to an unfortunate conflation of representation and represented:

1. his doctrine of ideas (like that of Locke's too) crammed too many distinct mental phenomena under one catch-all heading – after all, 'idea' in Locke's and Berkeley's usage covers concept and percept alike;
2. maybe Berkeley's rejection of abstract general ideas has blurred the distinction between the properties involved in the conception of an object and the properties of the object thereby conceived; and likewise;
3. as noted above, the force of this objection can be lessened somewhat if we bear in mind Berkeley's conceivability criterion of possibility.

However, making as much allowance as we reasonably can for points (1) to (3) above, there is a further problem: granted that conceivability determines possibility and that one of the cardinal abstractive errors is that of imagining a non-mental substance, why does Berkeley think we can form any conception of ideas which are perceived by minds other than our own? Many of the arguments Berkeley musters to establish that we cannot abstract the idea of mind from the idea of substance might seem to establish that we can't abstract from the idea of our perceptions to reach that of perception in general. Does the Master Argument not risk leading to solipsism?[31] However, to be fair to Berkeley, he never actually restricts the bounds of conceivable ideas to his own ideas and does (at least sometimes) seem to be open to the possibility that the same object can reside in different minds at once. As we shall hear later when discussing (§§135–47), Berkeley allows that while we can form no idea of other minds, we can form a notion of them and their perceptions. In this regard at least, other minds are no less accessible than our own – we can't perceive other minds (or their operations) but then again we can't perceive our own mind (and its operations) either, hence we must make shift as best we can with notions in both cases.

After Robinson (1996, introduction, pp. xxvii–xxix), one might try to elaborate on the Master Argument thus: we believe objects can exist externally to the mind, or at least externally to the particular mind that each of us possesses as an individual consciousness. Such 'externality' of the objects of perception is something we take for granted. However, if you believe that the only properties that ideas can have are those that can be presented to consciousness *and* you believe that the real objects of perception are those we directly perceive (as Berkeley did) you might be moved to wonder whence the idea of externality is derived. Of its very nature, the property of externality (i.e. of existing externally to the mind) is not the kind of property that can reside in an idea or that can be a possible object of perception. Likewise the property of 'existing without being perceived' cannot possibly be a property that we can perceive residing in any idea. And likewise again with the property of being a material substance. As we heard above, Berkeley makes important use of the Cartesian argument that all sensory appearances could be the same even though we were hallucinating or dreaming all the objects of our experience into existence. The importance of this Cartesian argument here is this: it is universally allowed that any appearances that the objects of our experience may present to us in normal perception are ones that they could also present to us in hallucinatory perception. Therefore, if all the properties that our ideas possess can be uncovered by our scrutiny, there cannot be any such thing as an impression of existing externally to the mind. Given the Cartesian premise that ideas can have the same apparent properties whether they are veridical or hallucinatory, if there was such an impression then our ideas could have the manifest property of external existence even while we were hallucinating. This would make this supposed impression of external existence a false impression. So external existence cannot *truly* be given to us as a manifest property of our ideas, and hence cannot be given to us via perception.[32] This interpretation has the advantage, among others, that it situates the Master Argument in the context of Berkeley's use of Cartesian sceptical arguments. (If it does nothing else, and it does a great deal else, Robinson's interpretation at least explains why the Master Argument of *PHK* §§22–3 follows so hard on the heels of the Cartesian 'dream' argument of *PHK* §§18–21.)

Still a feeling of dissatisfaction about the Master Argument remains even after all the above defences and counter-ploys have been considered. Perhaps the chief reason why the Master

Argument seems so uncompelling is that it presents a closed front to anyone not already of Berkeley's party. If we grant Berkeley that (1) conception involves representation, (2) representation is in turn constrained by likeness, and (3) only ideas can resemble (and hence represent) ideas, then we might grant him that the only conceivable entities are those (capable of) presentation to consciousness and that the only conceivable notion of existence is perception-dependent. However, anyone who has travelled thus far in granting Berkeley his premises is effectively a Berkeleyan *avant la lettre* and presumably shouldn't need the Master Argument to clinch the deal. The Master Argument needs a conceivability criterion of possibility and that criterion in turn needs a positive argument to establish why possibility must track conceivability.

§24 Having discussed the ontological status of ideas, we next come to their properties. Specifically, ideas can only exist in so far as they are perceived: 'For since they and every part of them exist only in the mind, it follows that there is nothing in them but what is perceived.' To further bolster the argument of §§22–3, Berkeley invites the reader to make a further exercise in experimental conception. This time, the conception that we are being asked to entertain is that of the '*absolute* [i.e. mind-independent] *existence of sensible objects*'. Now, the challenge is to conceive of the existence of a sensible object in a way that does not make reference to actual or possible perception. We should have already granted that sensible objects are merely collections of ideas, and that ideas cannot reside in an unthinking substance. Therefore, Berkeley says, we have to grant that the '*absolute existence of sensible objects*' is either meaningless or self-contradictory. However, this latest twist of the Master Argument seems susceptible to essentially the same objections as those outlined above.

Questions

1. What is the Master Argument designed to establish and is it successful?
2. Is Berkeley guilty of a crude fallacy in the Master Argument? If not, is he guilty of a sophisticated fallacy and what might this be?

3. Can the Master Argument be strengthened by appeal to a conceivability criterion of possibility?
4. Following J. L. Mackie (1976), does the Master Argument mistake an operational self-refutation for a genuine self-contradiction?

From the inertness of ideas to the existence of God (§§25–33)

Summary

The transparency of ideas (established in *PHK* 24) extends even to properties we would normally regard as epistemological or ontological. Inspecting our ideas reveal no impression of efficient causation or necessary connection, so ideas cannot be efficient causes or possess necessary connections with each other. If our ideas contain no more of active powers or efficient causality than we perceive them to have (namely, none), whatever joins ideas must operate at a level we cannot perceive.

Again, Berkeley invokes the 'Likeness Principle', whereby representation is restricted to resemblance and resemblance requires presentation to consciousness. Two utterly unlike things cannot enter into representational relationships, and active minds and passive ideas are too unlike for ideas to be able to represent minds. (Berkeley sometimes seems so convinced of the difference in mode of existence between minds and ideas that he even questions the propriety of applying the same word 'existence' to both of them, cf. *PHK* §89.) Ideas can resemble other ideas but as they lack all causal powers, they cannot generate other ideas and cannot organize themselves. Therefore only a mind can create associations between ideas.

The passivity of ideas is crucial to Berkeley's arguments for God's existence. We know our minds can create limited associations between ideas. (For example, the rules governing the English language allow us to create an association between the three-letter group 'CAT' and a kind of mammal. This association is mind-dependent, completely arbitrary and reflects no intrinsic affinities on the part of sign or signified. The word 'cat' bears no resemblance to its designated signifier.) Like an artificial language, the natural world exhibits associations between ideas, but of far greater scope and regularity than anything our minds could create. Therefore, a mind of superhuman power must exist. Berkeley's initial argument for God's existence (there will be another, with a slightly different tack, to be considered at §147) has two strands:

1. I can't choose to have any old perceptual ideas I please. Many ideas of perception are presented to me regardless of whether or not I will that they should be presented to me. Ideas are entirely *passive* and have nothing of active power in them (cf. *PHK* 25), therefore any generation of ideas must be done by something external to them. Ideas can only be caused by an active, agent intelligence, therefore there is something other than oneself (cf. *PHK* 29) and if I do not cause all of my perceptual ideas, and all causation is agency, then that something must be some other *agent* that causes my ideas. This first strand establishes that there is a transcendent agent. However, this strand of itself does not get us very close to the God of Christian orthodoxy or any form of theistic belief – the 'transcendent agent', for all we have heard so far, might be very powerful but completely indifferent or even actively hostile to our welfare – a sort of Berkeleyan 'evil demon'. (This lack of moral personality in the Great Agent will however be addressed in the next strand.)

2. The unmistakeable *order* and *continuity* we observe in our perceptions invite explanation in terms of something regulative which is external to those perceptions. Furthermore, Berkeley argues, the ideas we perceive show an order which invites comparison with the finest ordering we can observe in human artefacts, but exhibiting vastly greater sophistication and on a vastly greater scale. Thus, although God is transcendent, evidence of His purposes is not. Again if the only true causation is agency and the world's order manifestly transcends the power of any finite agent, then it follows that this order is due to an omnipotent (or at least vastly powerful) mind with (many of) the traditional attributes of God (*PHK* 30–2). (Although some gap remains between the God whose existence is thus established and the God of traditional theism.)

Section by section
§25 We now reach a crucial supplementary premise to Berkeley's reasoning, that is, that ideas are completely inert and possess no causal powers of their own at all. Again, we should be able to

recognize this truth purely by attending to our ideas. As argued before, ideas (and all their properties) exist only in the mind and they therefore can have no extra-perceptible properties. Attending to our own thoughts should be sufficient for us to determine whether or not ideas possess efficient causal powers, 'For since they and every part of them exist only in the mind, it follows that there is nothing in them but what is perceived.' Attending to the properties our ideas possess reveals no causal power in the ideas themselves; they 'are visibly inactive, there is nothing of power or agency included in them'. If ideas are passive, one idea cannot, of itself, generate or affect another idea. Neither can ideas represent anything but other ideas. Representation is restricted by resemblance, and ideas cannot resemble (hence cannot represent) anything imperceptible.

§26 Our ideas are continually changing – with new ones arising and old ones disappearing all the time. Something evidently must produce these ideas – but this something cannot itself be simply another (inert) idea. Having eliminated any possibility that ideas could reside in a material substance, Berkeley concludes that therefore there must be another spirit which is the cause of our ideas. (Berkeley doesn't consider here the possibility that ideas might arise purely spontaneously, without any earlier cause. It's hard to see how we could be *given* the impossibility of ideas arising spontaneously.)

§27 Spirit is one simple thing which, although single and undivided, can appear to us under different aspects. When perceiving ideas, it's called 'understanding' but when carrying out operations on (or with) ideas, spirit goes by the name 'will'. Spirit is active, where ideas are necessarily passive, hence (again by the Likeness Principle) it is impossible to form any idea of spirit or for any idea to represent a spirit: 'there can be no idea formed of a soul or spirit'.

At one pre-*PHK*, stage of his philosophical development, Berkeley thought minds might simply be collections of ideas.[33] Such a 'bundle' theory of the self was later to be seriously entertained by David Hume (1711–76). (Cf. *Treatise* I/IV/6, wherein Hume tells the bulk of humankind, that is, those who cannot follow certain metaphysicians in claiming to be able to perceive a continuous impression of the self, that 'they are nothing but a bundle or collection of different perceptions, which succeed each other with inconceivable rapidity, and are in a perpetual flux and movement'.) However, in later entries in the Commentaries and in all his published writings, Berkeley insists minds (or their operations) are not ideas, reducible to ideas or constructed out of ideas. (Cf. Berkeley's query to himself at *PC* 492 about whether or: 'not to call the operations of the mind ideas'.) Again, for spirits, existing is perceiving and not (unlike ideas) being perceived. Note another of Boswell's Dr Johnson anecdotes, this one from a collection of Johnsonian sayings made by Bennet Langton (the younger):

> Being in company with a gentleman who thought fit to maintain Dr. Berkeley's ingenious philosophy, that nothing exists but as perceived by some mind; when the gentleman was going away, Johnson said to him, 'Pray, sir, don't leave us; for we may perhaps forget to think of you, and then you will cease to exist.' (Boswell, 1791/1980, p. 1085)

This second Johnson anecdote illustrates how completely, and how quickly, the 'Esse est percipi' formulation came to overshadow 'Esse est percipi (aut percipere)' as the correct summary of Berkeley's metaphysics. Even if all Johnson's company stopped perceiving (or thinking of) the 'gentleman', he presumably kept on *perceiving* all the while. Note Berkeley is not simply saying that our *evidence* for the existence of mind is the mind's activity or that presentation to consciousness furnishes our evidence for the existence of objects. While Berkeley would accept these epistemic claims, he is also making two much stronger metaphysical claims: the existence of minds is literally *constituted* by their activity of perception just as the existence of objects is literally *constituted* by their being perceived. For unperceiving things, 'it is' is synonymous with 'it is perceived'; for perceiving things 'it is' is synonymous with 'it perceives'. (The Berkeleyan mind can therefore truly say: '*Percipio, ergo sum*', Luce, 1963, p. 123.) However, a charge often made against classical empiricism is that its proponents mistake the *epistemic* conditions that govern how we gain knowledge of something for the *metaphysical* conditions that are constitutive of that thing.

Now another Berkeleyan challenge to the reader's imaginative power: search your mind for any of: (1) an idea of active causal power, (2) the ideas of distinct powers separately called 'will' and 'understanding', and (3) a third idea, distinct from ideas (1) and (2), of some substance where these powers reside. (As usual, Berkeley is confident the reader's imaginative or introspective faculties will not rise to the task and that no such ideas as the above can be entertained.) However, while spirit cannot be perceived, we can still attach a meaning to the term 'spirit' and form some *notion* of the mind's operations. (The Berkeleyan notion of 'notion' will be returned to later, for example, at §89.)

§28 I have (at least some) voluntary control over my ideas. I can freely will that certain ideas be recalled to my consciousness, and immediately they are so. This voluntary summoning and dismissal of ideas is (partly) what makes the mind an agent and not merely a patient. Experience will verify the existence of such activity in the mind and reveal the incoherence (of the very idea) of 'unthinking agents'. Likewise incoherent is any notion that ideas could be generated without volition or use of the will. Where perception is passive and merely receives ideas, the imagination is active and can recombine existing ideas. We don't receive ideas and, while we may not be able to create ideas *ex nihilo* (this being a Divine prerogative), we can at least establish relations between them. (However, see *PC* 830: 'Why may we not conceive it possible for God to create things out of Nothing. certainly we our selves create in some wise whenever we imagine.')

§29 However, where ideas of the imagination depend (to a large extent) on my will, the same is not true of sensory ideas. My degree of freedom is much smaller when it comes to perceptual ideas. I can choose whether or not to open my eyes but I can't choose not to see if I do open my eyes and I can't choose what I will see if I do open my eyes.

§30 In addition, ideas of sense are stronger, livelier and more distinct than ideas of imagination. Ideas of sense show a stability, order and coherence that ideas of imagination often lack. So, Berkeley holds, where ideas of the imagination (or illusion) arise at random and follow no discernible order, ideas of sense show a continuing stability and reliability. We observe that ideas of sense fall into patterns and regular successions. (As will become apparent later, Berkeley holds that the laws of nature are thus the rules whereby the external spirit produces and regulates our ideas.)

§31 The stability of natural laws allows us to make plans for the future and to regulate our expectations, hence provides more evidence of the wisdom and benevolence of the great spirit that regulates the world of sensible things. (The God-given nature of the regularity of Nature, and the prospects it offer us of planning our course through life, will be significant when we come to look at Berkeley's response to the problem of evil in §§151–3.)

§32 Strangely (and unfortunately) the very stability of natural laws is something that we take so much for granted that we tend to forget that God is solely and ultimately responsible for the regularity in Nature that makes our lives possible. Instead, through mere habit and by a strange process of transference, we attribute causal powers to objects themselves, treating them as 'secondary causes'. This is absurd – ideas (or combinations of ideas) cannot be the cause of other ideas, or exhibit any causal powers at all.

§33 By now the reader may be thinking: well, if everything that exists does so exclusively inside some mind or other, what possible difference can there be between the existence of real objects and delusionary ones? If we wish to say that a pain, for example, is largely the invention of its alleged sufferer, we might tell said sufferer that 'It's all in the mind.' Common sense certainly seems to assume that real objects exist outside the mind whereas delusionary 'objects' exist solely within the mind and needn't resemble real things at all. Berkeley of course has to grant that both kinds of objects (like all objects) exist within the mind. It isn't where objects reside that makes them real or illusory. However he offers three ways of distinguishing sensible ideas (i.e. ideas of real things) from ideas of imagination (i.e. ideas of chimerical things). First, ideas of sense are less amenable to voluntary summoning or dismissal on our part, whereas ideas of imagination can be conjured up or dismissed at will. (Although of course certain disturbances of the imagination or the mind can create chimerical ideas that the mind cannot banish at will.) Secondly, ideas of imagination are less vivid and stable than sensible ideas. Thirdly, sensible ideas show far greater mutual coherence and continuity than the ideas of the imagination. Berkeley could also claim that the collections of ideas that constitute physical objects present consistent appearances, whether to the several senses of one percipient, and/or the senses of several percipients. (Although bear in mind that the different senses don't literally perceive the same objects – tactile ideas are tactile ideas, visual ideas are visual ideas and these kinds are necessarily distinct. The link between the ideas of the different senses is one of association and regular conjunction in experience.) Consider literature's greatest hallucinatory object, the dagger that appears floating before Macbeth's eyes as he hesitates over killing King Duncan. Macbeth addresses the dagger thus:

> Is this a dagger which I see before me,
> The handle toward my hand? Come, let me clutch thee.
> I have thee not, and yet I see thee still.
> Art thou not, fatal vision, sensible
> To feeling as to sight? or art thou but
> A dagger of the mind, a false creation,
> Proceeding from the heat-oppress'd brain?
> (*Macbeth*, Act 2, sc. 1, ll. 33–9)

What alerts Macbeth to the dagger's unreality is that it yields ideas only to his eyes and not his hand, that is, it's because the dagger is a purely visual dagger that Macbeth concludes it's a 'dagger of the mind'. Had the dagger been (1) sensible to Macbeth's touch and/or (2) visible to others, then it might be a real dagger, albeit one suspended in the air. (Macbeth seems to be a thorough Berkeleyan when it comes to sifting veridical from hallucinatory perceptions.)

Woolhouse (Introduction to *PHK/D*, 1988, p. 15) points out that Locke and Descartes also used the above criteria for distinguishing real from chimerical objects.[34] This is an interesting strategy for them to adopt, because all three criteria above are *internal* to the agent's perceptions, that is, the percipient can judge how far ideas match these criteria without appeal to external features like the ideas' causes. Being materialists, Locke and Descartes could have appealed to external conditions, like differences in the causal origins of real and chimerical ideas, to distinguish veridical from illusory perception.

Berkeley later noted this similarity between immaterialist and materialist ways for spotting chimerical ideas: 'In short, by whatever method you distinguish *things* from *chimeras* on your own scheme, the same, it is evident, will hold also upon mine. For it must be, I presume, by some perceived difference and I am not for depriving you of any one thing that you perceive' (*D* 235).

So, Berkeley concludes, ideas of imagination can correctly be called images or copies of the sensible objects that they represent. However, real things are simply those collections of ideas which show the greater degree of coherence, will-independence, vividness and stability. However, such real things are nonetheless collections of ideas of sensation and 'are nevertheless *ideas*, that is, they exist in the mind, or are perceived by it, as truly as the ideas of its own framing' (original emphasis). However, while ideas of sensation do not show the same dependence on our will for their existence, they must still, being ideas, be dependent on some will and specifically, a will vastly more powerful than ours. (Notice how gently, without mentioning God explicitly, Berkeley introduces the notion of a vastly powerful spirit whose purposes issue in the stability and coherence of the ideas of sensation.) So, the difference between real things and imaginary things is that the ideas composing the former are more stable and vivid, and far less dependent on the will of the human percipient.

Questions

1. Can we infer that ideas are inert from their lack of observable causal powers?
2. Are perceptual ideas truly inert? After all, surely if a spot in my visual field is green, this precludes that same area being red – would this be an instance of a causal power possessed by (in this case visual) ideas?
3. Assuming Berkeley shows that ideas can't be causes in their own right, does he also establish that collections of ideas can't be causes either? Would a demonstration that ideas (taken individually) possess no causal powers suffice to show that ideas taken collectively couldn't possess causal powers either? Is there a risk of a 'fallacy of composition' here?
4. Does Berkeley really have a sustainable criterion for distinguishing between real and delusory sensory experiences?

5. A familiar science fiction trope is the virtual reality simula-
tion. Virtual reality seems to allow the possibility of shared
access to sensible objects, but for limited groups of people.[35]
What might Berkeley make of objects made in virtual
realities?

PHILOSOPHICAL OBJECTIONS TO
IMMATERIALISM, AND REPLIES (§§34–81)
Common sense and idealism (§§34–49)

Summary
From roughly §34 to §81, Berkeley considers philosophical
objections to idealism and offers replies. (Before doing so, he
apologizes if he overinsists on points that may seem obvious
to the reader, but craves pardon on the grounds that people's
powers of apprehension differ. I beg the reader's pardon
likewise.)

Berkeley repeatedly testified that he believed, wholeheartedly, in the existence of all the objects of common sense belief.
He was adamant that he did not dispute or deny the existence
of a solitary thing admitted by common sense. When he denies
the existence of an imperceptible, mind-independent material
substance, this alleged something is an entity that no one but
philosophers believe in. 'Matter' is something common sense
opinion doesn't accept and would not miss. In general, Berkeley
acclaimed common sense against philosophical oversubtlety.

However, some of his claims seem at variance with common
sense, notably his famous claim about the identity of perception
and existence. Common sense seemingly thinks the existence
of physical objects is neither identical with, nor implies, their
being perceived. Common sense allows existing physical things
which aren't perceived and which may never be perceived. I
can now see my desk, my computer and various pens, so these
objects seem both existent and perceived. However, while I cannot now perceive the enclosed interior of my desk, I presume its
contents still exist although currently unperceived. Indeed, we
usually think objects can exist even if no one ever perceives
them. I'm told Sirius B is a white dwarf star apparently composed of compressed matter many times denser than Earthly
materials. Human beings may never observe what goes on at

Sirius B's core but common sense would allow that Sirius B's core could still exist, even if forever unperceived.

Berkeley challenges our (alleged) common sense willingness to accept unperceived objects in two ways. First, he disputes that common sense does allow unperceivable objects. Berkeley says: if you entertain the thought that an object exists, you can only do so by imagining the object as a possible object of perception. As we heard above when discussing the Master Argument, Berkeley thinks that to frame the idea of a thing as existing is precisely to frame the idea of that thing as perceptible. The only possible existents are objects of (perceptually based) imagination and entities who exercise perceptual powers – that is, ideas or minds. In imagining Sirius B's core, you imagine it as it *would be perceived*. Secondly, Berkeley (1) holds finite minds are not the only kind in existence and (2) thinks humans may not be the only finite spirits in existence. Even if no human ever perceives the core of Sirius B, Sirius B's core may nonetheless be perceived – by God's omnipresent perception and/or by finite, non-human spirits. We can't safely infer that just because something can't be perceived by human beings, that it can't be perceived by God or other spirits. (However, not even God can perceive a logically impossible being.) Being unperceived by all human beings need not be the same as being unperceived *tout court*. Anyway, even if Berkeley's rejection of perception-independent existence is at odds with common sense, he would claim that idealism is relatively more commonsensical than materialism (even if not absolutely so). Berkeley's idealism might still be less revisionary of common sense than the materialist representationalism about perception of Locke, Descartes or Malebranche.

Berkeley considers several objections to idealism from everyday reasoning. First, he tackles the objection that idealism makes every substantial existent dissolve into mere illusion. Berkeley replies that he does not deny the existence of anything perceptible; what he is concerned to deny is that any imperceptible substance underlies what we perceive. Idealism doesn't threaten the 'substantiality' of chairs, tables or mountains. Nor does Berkeley's philosophy deny that such objects possess extension, weight and solidity – however, it does remove any need to posit an imperceptible substratum that somehow supports these qualities.

To support his claim to be upholding common sense, Berkeley (*PHK* 37) distinguishes between *vulgar* and *philosophical* uses of words. It is only the philosophers' conception of material substance that he seeks to deny. While it may sound odd to say that we eat ideas, drink ideas and are clothed and warmed by ideas, the oddity diminishes if we consider that the real things spoken of by the vulgar are no more than collections of ideas. In a nutshell, rather than downgrade things to the status of 'mere' ideas, Berkeley wishes to elevate ideas (or collections of ideas) to the status of things.

In Berkeley's system, physical objects can exist whether or not any human mind happens to perceive them. Berkeley need not claim that physical objects have a discontinuous existence – they needn't flit out of existence once our backs are turned and flit back again when we resume perceiving them. However, Berkeley does insist that physical objects cannot exist without being *in some way* perceived. So, Berkeley would accept that the chair I'm sitting on now would still exist if I left the room and stopped perceiving it. Indeed, he would accept that my chair would still exist even if no human beings at all were perceiving it. However, he would deny that my chair could still exist if cut off from all perception whatsoever. Objects require (at least the possibility of) somebody perceiving them if they are to exist. Whether the perception concerned is actual or merely possible, sensible (hence) physical objects must be related to perception.

Section by section

§34 *First objection*: doesn't immaterialism remove everything solid and enduring in existence, and leave only an assembly of 'chimerical' and transitory ideas? The immaterialist doctrine seems to threaten our beliefs in the integrity of every single physical thing. ('What therefore becomes of the sun, moon and stars? What must we think of houses, rivers, mountains, trees, stones; nay even of our own bodies?') Berkeley replies that his doctrine does not threaten the existence of any portion of the natural world nor does it threaten the existence of the natural world itself. As noted above, for all that chimerical and real existents must be composed of ideas, there remains a principled distinction between real and delusionary experience.

§35 Berkeley takes pains here to emphasize that he is not try-ing to deny the existence of a single sensible object or *object of reflection*. (This last is a significant addition.) He does not dispute that, for example, the objects we apprehend by sight or touch do genuinely exist. Rather than *remove* any of the objects of common sense, instead all he wishes to deny is the existence of that thing hypothesized by philosophers which is called 'matter' or 'material substance'. Common sense won't lose anything if material substance is argued out of existence, because common sense never really believed in such a thing in the first place. Only two kinds of people will suffer any loss in the abandonment of material substance: (1) the atheist will lose 'the colour of an empty name to support his impiety' (i.e. the metaphysical nullity at the core of atheism will be more easily revealed) and (2) philosophers will lose a great way of generat-ing endless inconsequential disputes. ('And', one feels Berkeley is sorely tempted to add, 'I frankly don't care about *these* incon-veniences to *these* people'.) Common sense, however, will not notice any change if material substance is abandoned, because common sense is closer to (idealist) direct realism.

§36 By now, Berkeley says, if you *still* think immaterialism denies the existence of any object whose existence is normally countenanced by common sense, then you haven't understood his doctrine correctly. (Indeed, as Berkeley thinks he has stated his doctrine in 'the plainest terms' he can think of, the hint is clear: if you haven't got it by now, it's your fault and cannot be attributed to excessive technicality or abstruse language on Berkeley's part.) He summarizes his doctrine anew: human spirits (or souls) can perceive for themselves that they can cre-ate or remove their ideas of reflection at will. However, they can also perceive that their ideas of sense are not dependent on their wills. The ideas of imagination can be seen to be faint and changeable, whereas the ideas of the senses are steady, reli-able and law like. We can count on the ideas of sense. Indeed, Berkeley says (and this is a slightly puzzling turn of phrase for him to adopt) the ideas of sense 'have more *reality* in them' (ori-ginal emphasis – cf. §33). He seems to mean that sensory ideas are more affecting than the ideas of imagination – the former have a more powerful grip on our attention and have greater staying-power than the latter. What you can see in the sky during the day is the real Sun; what you can imagine by night is the idea of the Sun.

§37 Surely though, it cannot be denied that immaterialism at least banishes 'corporeal substance' from existence, if nothing else. Well, says Berkeley in effect, it all depends on what you mean by 'corporeal substance'. If 'corporeal substance' means a really existing combination of qualities like extension, solidity and weight, then no, the charge that immaterialism banishes substance is completely false. In this common sense (or 'vulgar') acceptation of the term, 'corporeal substance' is in no danger from immaterialism – the immaterialist is genuinely convinced that there are really existing objects that combine properties like solidity, extension and weight. However, there is another, 'philosophical sense' of substance. If, as (materialist) philosophers seemingly do, you intend 'substance' to refer to an imperceptible substratum that supports the qualities that we perceive but which itself is nothing like any perceptible object, then the existence of *this* kind of substance is something that Berkeley does emphatically deny. However, this loss is easily borne, since the immaterialist is only 'taking away' something that could never have existed in the first place. If 'physical object' denotes something that possesses properties like density, colour, shape, texture, sound and smell, then Berkeley believed wholeheartedly in physical objects.

§38 Surely though, Berkeley's opponent might continue, immaterialism does at least do violence to our ordinary ways of talking and produces results that sound nonsensical or at least utterly strange: 'it sounds very harsh to say we eat and drink ideas, and are clothed with ideas'. Berkeley attributes this apparent clumsiness or uncouthness in so talking to the fact that we don't ordinarily refer to things as being combinations of ideas and anything that goes against our ordinary usage will sound peculiar (at least at first). Here, ordinary language does enshrine a philosophical mistake. If we were already in the habit of calling collections of sensory ideas (i.e. real things) by the more accurate name of 'ideas', then we would feel far less uneasiness in saying that we eat, drink and are clothed by, ideas. However, what matters is not whether or not a given usage sounds pleasing to the ear but whether or not it's philosophically correct, and combinations of sensible ideas are just precisely what real things actually are. Provided we grant that we are fed, drink and clothed in the 'immediate objects of sense', Berkeley grants that it is probably closer to ordinary usage to call them 'things'.

§39 Why then does Berkeley not use the word 'thing' more readily? Why does he call the immediate objects of experience 'ideas'? Berkeley offers two reasons, both rooted in ordinary usage: (1) 'Thing' is often taken to mean something that exists outside the mind; and (2) 'Thing' is often used to refer to more entities than just ideas, that is, minds can be called 'things' too. So, to keep clear that the immediate objects of sense are first, mind-dependent and secondly, inactive, Berkeley prefers calling them 'ideas' rather than 'things'.

§40 Berkeley then imagines a critic replying that the evidence of the senses will always prevail against argument, however plausible, and that the evidence of the senses favours the externality (i.e. mind-independence or 'absolute existence') of objects. Now, Berkeley goes some way with this critic, in that he allows that the evidence of the senses is ordinarily utterly compelling. Indeed, he goes so far as to affirm that he believes in the real existence of the things he sees, feels and hears as readily as he believes in his own existence. (This last is a rather un-Cartesian thought. Descartes of course famously held that while scepticism about the existence of any or all perceived objects was at least coherent, the existence of the thinking self is incapable of being coherently doubted and thus is on a quite different level of certainty from any fact derived from the evidence of our senses.) Berkeley also allows that the testimony of the senses decisively favours the existence of sensible objects. However, what Berkeley denies is that perceptual evidence can support the *mind-independent* existence of objects. (As before, the senses cannot furnish any idea of any relationship that our ideas of sense might have with anything imperceptible.) Berkeley again affirms that his arguments are the reverse of sceptical or distrustful about the evidence of the senses. If we believe instead that 'real' things somehow lie behind what we perceive, then we risk scepticism. All that lies beneath or behind the world of sensory experience is not some mind-independent substance or substratum but another mental realm, that of God's ideas and purposes. (It is the continuity of God's purposes that ensures that we continue to perceive a stable, predictable and regular world.)

§41 *Second objection*: we all believe that a vast gulf separates our merely having an idea (or dreaming) of fire from the real tangible fire that can actually burn us. Berkeley's reply is perhaps a little too quick for easy grasping but essentially his argument is the same as in previous sections: we can only observe the relations between the fire we perceive and the burning we feel. At no time, can we observe a relationship between, for example, the burning sensation and some imperceptible cause.

§42 *Third objection*: we can actually perceive distance directly and so we can tell that many of the objects we perceive are at a distance from us, and hence cannot be inside the mind. It seems absurd then to claim that things whose remoteness from ourselves is directly perceivable, should nonetheless be supposed to exist inside our minds (in among our thoughts as it were). Berkeley's initial reply to objection 3: there is no necessary connection between an object seeming to be at a distance from us and it's actually being so. (In dreams, we seem to see things that lie at a great distance from us, although they are really within the mind.)

§43 Berkeley's second reply to objection 3: in fact, we do *not* really perceive distance directly at all. Berkeley refers the reader to his earlier *NTV*, especially §41. In this work, he argues that distance is not an immediately perceivable thing or something we can judge by its necessary connections with other properties, but rather something we learn to infer from a set of cues. We cannot perceive the geometrical relations that our eyes make with visual objects and distance (or depth) itself is not directly perceptible, being 'a line directed end-wise to the eye' (*NTV* 2). Hence, in Berkeley's terminology, distance can only be *mediately* perceived via its attendant signs, not *immediately* perceived via direct presentation to consciousness. In mediate perception, one idea is perceived by means of another idea. We learn to correlate certain visual ideas with certain tactile ones, and that is how we learn to grasp the concept of distance. For example, we notice that objects occupy less of the visual field and that their colours get fainter as they are placed at a greater (tactilely perceived) distance from us. We can also grasp distance via the associated tactile ideas of strain and differential focusing derived from the changing visual axes of the eyes.

§44 Rather than being necessarily linked together, the ideas we derive from the sense of sight and those we derive from the sense of touch are of completely different kinds. The ideas of sight are signs for the associated ideas of touch. Berkeley appeals here to results already established in his *NTV*, since in *NTV* Berkeley established (at least to his own satisfaction) that all visual objects exist entirely within the mind. In connection with Berkeley's (*NTV* and later) views on distance perception, consider the famous 'Molyneux problem', first posed in a 1793 letter to Locke by William Molyneux (1656–98), and incorporated by Locke into the second edition of his *Essay*. Molyneux asked whether a congenitally blind person, newly given sight, could recognize visually objects known hitherto only by touch:

> Suppose a Man born blind, and now adult, and taught by his touch to distinguish between a Cube, and a Sphere of the same metal, and nighly of the same bigness, so as to tell, when he felt one and t'other, which is the Cube, which the Sphere. Suppose then the Cube and Sphere placed on a Table, and the Blind Man to be made to see. Quære, Whether by his sight, before he touch'd them, he could now distinguish, and tell, which is the Globe, which the Cube. (*Essay* II/ix/8)

To this question, Locke and Berkeley both answered 'no' – no necessity associates the ideas given to us by different senses and only experience will reveal which tactile ideas relate to which visual shapes. Of Molyneux's erstwhile blind person, Berkeley writes: 'He would not consider the ideas of sight with reference to, or as having any connection with, the ideas of touch: his view of them being entirely terminated within themselves' (*NTV* 79). Furthermore, no necessity links visual ideas to 'outwardness' or existence external to the mind: 'A man born blind, being made to see, would, at first, have no idea of distance by sight; the sun and stars . . . would all seem to be in his eye, or rather in his mind' (*NTV* 41).[36]

§45 *Fourth objection*: surely if all the objects we perceive depend on being perceived for their existence, it seems to follow inevitably that objects must cease to exist and be re-created again every moment (i.e. that perceived objects must have a discontinuous existence).

§46 Berkeley now offers two replies to objection 4: (1) A *tu quoque* response: other philosophical positions besides immaterialism are committed to the periodic non-existence of the immediate objects of perception, so Berkeley is no worse off in this regard than his opponents. If you are a representationalist about perception, you still have to admit that the objects you immediately perceive have an intermittent existence. For example, all the visual ideas of light and colours you receive of a tree must cease to exist when you close your eyes. When you open your eyes again, new visual ideas of the tree spring into being that somehow manage to resemble the now-vanished ideas you had previously. (2) In any event, continuous creation may not be so very counter-intuitive after all. Other philosophers have accepted such a doctrine. Those Scholastic philosophers who believed in matter nonetheless held that it could only be held in being by God's preserving it and that such 'divine conservation . . . . By them is expounded to be a continual creation'. Luce (1963, pp. 32–6, citing *PC* 830) argues that Berkeley considered *but rejected* the doctrine of intermittent existence for unthinking things before ever he wrote *PHK*. So: the task for the mature (*PHK*) Berkeley was to explain in what way merely perceivable things exist.

The problem prompts several questions. What is the status of objects that are not currently perceived by humans and are therefore perceived only by God? Can the same perceptual objects be present to God's consciousness and to ours? Assuming that God must make use of sensory intermediaries like sight or touch in order to grasp objects seems to diminish God's power (and to anthropomorphize God). Berkeley did not accept that in perceiving objects (or their properties) we literally access the contents of God's consciousness or somehow share the ideas God perceives. (Although Malebranche held this.) Two views suggest themselves: one 'idealist' and the other 'phenomenalist'. Bennett distinguishes the two doctrines thus: phenomenalism holds *'Objects are logical constructions out of sense data'* (Bennett, 1971, p. 137), where idealism holds *'Objects are collections of sense data'* (Bennett, p. 138).

The 'idealist' Berkeley would hold that God maintains in existence those objects we don't currently perceive by having ideas of a similar kind to ours but on a vastly greater scale. (As though God's perception of a chair contrives to be a non-perspectival, all-encompassing perception of an object that we humans can perceive only fragmentarily and transitorily.) On this view, our perceptual ideas and those of God are at least entities of broadly the same kind, even if God's ideas are inconceivably more detailed and richer than our own. (Although this interpretation risks anthropomorphism, in making God's perceptions qualitatively similar to ours.) The 'phenomenalist' Berkeley would hold that God need not have perceptual ideas that resemble ours in any way, but instead achieves the continuity of our perceptions by ensuring that the world of sensory ideas remains consistent over interruptions in our perception. On this view, God ensures the chair I perceive when I come back into my office after a short absence is qualitatively similar to the chair I perceived before I popped out, but God need not have been having perceptual ideas which are qualitatively similar to mine during my absence. (Berkeley seems to have at least contemplated a phenomenalist solution to the unperceived perceivables problem in *PHK*.)

Although often described as an anti-realist doctrine about physical objects, phenomenalism does not deny that physical objects exist. As Michael Dummett puts it, phenomenalism is not best characterized as the view that material objects either don't exist or that names of material objects don't refer, but rather as the view that material objects are *logical constructions* out of sense-data.[37] Thus, claims about physical objects are to be analysed as claims about what sort of sense-data different sets of circumstances might bring forth. With phenomenalism, claims about unperceived perceivable objects can be analysed using subjunctive conditionals about what we would perceive if different circumstances obtained.[38] (Thus, such objects themselves would thus be something like the constitutive grounds of 'permanent possibilities of sensation'.[39]) For example, I am not currently able to verify by direct sensory perception whether or not there are penguins in the South Atlantic. However, a penguin seems an eminently perceivable object so presumably if I were placed in the right circumstances, I would perceive penguins. Thus, the phenomenalist analysis of the statement 'There are penguins in the South Atlantic' involves a coun- terfactual, for example, 'If I were placed in the right sort of location in the South Atlantic then I would see penguins.' This preserves the link to perception without restricting existence to the actually perceived.

So which is best for Berkeley – idealism or phenomenalism about the unperceived? When it comes to unperceived but per- ceivable objects, idealism seems to have three options: (1) things that aren't currently perceived by humans remain present to another mind; (2) objects flit in and out of existence when not perceived; (3) objects cease to exist once perception stops but qualitatively indistinguishable objects pop into existence to fill their places once perception resumes. These two latter options prompt questions about how coherent it is to imagine one and the same object having a discontinuous existence or why the objects that appear once perception resumes manage to mimic so closely the originals that were destroyed when perception ceased.

However, phenomenalism allows unperceived but perceiv- able objects without any commitment as to whether or not the unperceived perceivables exist in a state similar to that in which perceived perceivables exist.[40] Thus, for theist phenomenalists, God can guarantee the existence of currently unperceived per- ceivable objects by making the right counterfactuals come out true but not necessarily by having perceptual ideas which resem- ble ours. If the existence of perceivable objects is underwritten by the continuity of God's purposes, these are clearly mental existents and thus compatible with an idealist/immaterialist ontology. On this view, the linkage between God as guarantor of perception and the nature of natural laws is thus: 'the existence of the physical world is reduced to the organization which, by his volitional strategy, God imposes on human experience' (Foster and Robinson (eds), 1985, Introduction, p. 10). This interpret- ation is more phenomenalist than idealist in spirit. (Foster and Robinson (ibid.) argue that this phenomenalist interpretation is the one Berkeley had in mind while writing *PHK*, but that he had switched to an 'idealist' conception of unperceived existence by the time he composed *D*.) Besides removing any commit- ment to our somehow sharing God's ideas, this phenomenalist analysis also fits with Berkeley's own remarks about the 'books in the closet' case (*PHK* 23). There, Berkeley seems to accept that talk about the existence of currently unperceived perceivables can be analysed as talk about what we would perceive if our circumstances were different. In a nutshell, phenomenalism (as opposed to idealism) about unperceived physical objects has several advantages for the Berkeleyan:

1. Gives an account of the actual/possible objects distinction.
2. Allows a role for scientific investigation of microstructure and hence microscopy. (See §§60–2)
3. Means the archetypal ideas eternally present in God's understanding need not qualitatively resemble the ideas we (fleetingly and fragmentarily) perceive.[41]

§47 Another reply to objection 4: As noted above (in §46), on any conception, the objects we perceive must cease to exist when they aren't being perceived. However, any philosophical belief in material substance is in a worse case than any other view because this view is already committed to the doctrine that real objects must have properties demonstrably distinct from those of perceived objects.

§48 Still another reply to objection 4, and perhaps the most fundamental of all: for all that ideas exist only when being perceived, we cannot safely infer that just because ideas cease to be perceived by any human being, that they must therefore cease to have all existence whatsoever. For all we know, those objects that we cease to perceive may remain in existence through being perceived by another spirit. While Berkeley does accept that existence involves perception by some mind, it does not follow that the objects I perceive only exist when I perceive them. (Existence in my mind is not after all the only possible way of existing, nor are human minds necessarily the only kind there are. Therefore, an object might still exist even if it were present to no human consciousness at all.) Berkeley points out that the kind of mind-independent existence he denies is existence independent of any mind whatsoever; he is happy to accept that objects may exist independently of any particular (finite) mind. (Although in this section Berkeley does not explicitly mention the possibility of infinite mind, that is, God, it is quite clear from other remarks that he clearly believed that finite minds need not be the only kind of minds there are. Indeed, besides finite human minds and God's infinite mind, Berkeley's system did allow that there may be other kinds of finite minds besides ours, for example, angels.) Hence from the truth of immaterialism and the perception-dependent nature of existence, it need not follow that objects have an intermittent existence.

§49 *Fifth objection*: If then the so-called primary qualities (like shape and extension) exist only within the mind, then this seemingly has the absurd consequence that the mind itself must be extended and have a shape (or shapes). However, this conclusion needs the additional premise that extension is 'a mode or attribute, which . . . is predicated of the subject in which it exists'. (This doctrine, which Berkeley attributes to the Schoolmen, that is, medieval or medievally inspired Scholastic philosophers, was also accepted by Malebranche. However, in Malebranche's system, the secondary qualities are modes or modifications of finite minds, while the primary qualities exist as modes of God's mind.[42]) Berkeley's reply is that extension does not exist in the mind as a mode (or modification) or attribute of the mind but rather as an *idea* in it. (This is a significant distinction for Berkeley to draw, since it suggests that he was at least aware of the dangers inherent in attributing too hastily the properties of the thing represented to that which does the representation. That Berkeley was at least aware of this distinction, and also diagnosed a failure to observe it in his Scholastic opponents, might have a bearing on the interpretation of the Master Argument of §§22–3. See above on the alleged 'grotesque fallacy' reading of the Master Argument.)

Questions
1. Why does Berkeley claim not to threaten the existence of a single object of reflection? Is the existence of objects of reflection in danger of eroding the distinction between veridical and hallucinatory perception?
2. Does 'phenomenalism' or 'idealism' do the better job of explaining God's role in preserving sensible objects? If the Berkeleyan embraces phenomenalism, how might counterfactual conditionals about perceivables be analysed?
3. In view of his remarks on continuous creation at §46, should Berkeley simply have chosen to bite the bullet and just accept

that physical objects only exist intermittently? Would this be an insuperable objection to his version of idealism?

4. Is the postulation of finite but non-human percipients just an *ad hoc* manoeuvre on Berkeley's part or does it command some independent philosophical (as opposed to theological) justification?

5. How might Berkeley distinguish between an idea like, for example, extension existing in the mind as a mode and its existing in the mind as an idea?

6. Does Berkeley show any evidence of properly grasping the distinction between the properties of the representation and the properties of the represented?

Ordinary language and efficient causation (§§50–3)

Summary

With Locke and Hume, Berkeley maintains that we do not perceive necessary connections between ideas. However, for Berkeley, there is a force which joins ideas together apart from their associations in our mind, namely God's *fiat*. (So Berkeley thought there was a transcendental explanation for the correlation of ideas, but no necessity resides in the ideas themselves.) Berkeley not only makes our experience of volition the model for causation, but assimilates all efficient causality to agency. However, in ordinary life, we say, for example, 'The fire burned my hand', as though efficient causation resides in the fire and not the Divine agent behind our ideas of fire. Berkeley tried to respect normal usage wherever possible. He knew his theory denied efficient causality in matter but insisted we could retain useful everyday speech about causality even though strictly speaking there is only agency. However ordinary usages should be retained unless they are dangerously misleading. Whether or not Berkeley's idealism reflects ordinary usage, he did not seek to replace everyday language with a logically refined alternative. His empiricism may have been rigorous but he was not a logical positivist.

Section by section

§50 *Sixth objection*: Physical science seems to require the postulation of material objects and can explain many phenomena using this hypothesis. Indeed, modern science and philosophy would collapse if the 'corpuscular' hypothesis was disallowed. Berkeley replies that the apparent explanatory success of corpuscularianism is really nothing of the kind, since there is no attestable instance where corpuscularian explanation has succeeded where immaterialism cannot do an equally good explanatory job. He argues that explanation is effectively the same as showing 'why upon such and such occasions we are affected by such and such ideas'. However, as remarked on before, it is completely mysterious how matter could so act on the mind as to produce ideas therein. (Again, a difficulty for interactionist dualists like Descartes was the apparent unintelligibility of any causal mechanism that could bridge the gulf between material and mental substance.) Hence the postulation of matter as an explanation for the occurrence or properties of our ideas is completely useless. Furthermore, the corpuscularians themselves don't really explain the phenomena we observe by reference to corporeal *substance* (i.e. the alleged imperceptible substratum beneath appearances) but rather by reference to *qualities* that are meant to inhere in this substance – qualities like extension, solidity and motion. These qualities (as Berkeley would maintain he has already demonstrated) are only ideas, and we know no idea can possess causal powers and therefore cannot be the cause of any other idea. (Here, Berkeley refers to §25.)

In defending the coherence of mental causation, Berkeley can also appeal to the link between agency and understanding. Agent causation requires volitions, which in turn require ideas and must therefore possess content. An agent must possess an idea of that which it causes. So, any exterior causes of our perceptions must exist in another *mind*, but a mind of much greater power than ours. So, for Berkeley, there is at least a valid inference *from* the independence of exterior objects *to* their continuing in existence when we aren't perceiving them. Where we get the very idea of continuity from (and how we might justify it) is another story.[43]

§51 *Seventh objection*: Denying natural causation in objects and instead ascribing all causation to 'the immediate operation of spirits' is absurd. We certainly talk as though causal powers resided in objects themselves – we attribute heating to fire and cooling to water, and don't make any reference to spirit in such cases. If we were speaking strictly (for philosophical purposes) we ought really to say not 'that fire heats, or water cools, but that a spirit heats, and so forth'. Someone who tried to replace ordinary usage in these cases by talking of a spirit heating would rightly deserve ridicule. Berkeley replies with the admonition that 'in such things, we ought to *"think with the learned, and speak with the vulgar"*'.[44] After all, we still talk of sunrise and sunset centuries after Copernicus established that actually it's the Earth that rotates and not the Sun that rises and falls. This usage is so well entrenched that using the more philosophically correct terms would sound absurd. If at all possible, ordinary usage ought to be respected where it isn't guilty of gross error and/or where reformed usage would be cumbersome. In any case, Berkeley maintains that immaterialism, properly understood, does no violence to common sense notions.

§52 Further to §51: usages can be retained which we know to be strictly speaking false: 'In the ordinary affairs of life, any phrases may be retained, so long as they excite in us proper sentiments, or dispositions to act in such a manner as is necessary for our well-being, how false soever they be, if taken in a strict and speculative sense.' Indeed, some flexibility and generosity in interpreting ordinary usage are virtues, since language must adapt itself to custom and 'received opinions', which won't always be of the utmost philosophical accuracy. It isn't therefore to be expected that any philosophical doctrine will be perfectly unambiguous and (therefore) immune from leaving scope for carping criticism. (Note Berkeley's doctrine of interpretative tolerance also fits with at least a limited non-ideational theory of meaning. A word or phrase can still be useful and admissible into speech even if it doesn't arouse the correct ideas or images in our minds, provided that it conduces to the production of correct sentiments and conduct.)

§53 Returning to the falsity of corpuscularianism: the doctrine of the causal impotence of matter is not a newfangled invention of Berkeley's but one that can be traced back to medieval philosophers, who thought 'God alone to be the immediate cause of all things'. The doctrine Berkeley has in mind is often called 'occasionalism' and, while associated particularly with Nicolas Malebranche, is actually a much older doctrine, and was upheld by other Cartesians, including Claude Clerselier (1614–84), and

Louis de la Forge (1632–66). Malebranche's forerunners in the denial of material causation include the Islamic theologian Abu Hamid al-Ghazali (1058–1111) and the Andalusian Jewish philosopher Solomon ibn Gabirol (c. 1021–c. 1058).[45] Deriving from Neoplatonic roots, medieval occasionalists thought (1) all matter is casually inert, (2) efficient causation resides only in God and cannot be delegated to created beings, and hence (3) matter is only an occasion that God's infinite agency uses to produce effects. Other medieval philosophers (e.g. Moses Maimonides (1138–1204) and Thomas Aquinas), rejected occasionalism.

Questions
1. Granted interactionism has problems accounting for the link between our volitions and our movements, can idealism fare any better?
2. How much violence does Berkeleyan idealism do to our common sense conceptions of (a) existence and (b) causation? If Berkeley's idealism does run contrary to common sense, is this a price worth paying?
3. If we were to adopt a Berkeleyan view of causation in our everyday speech, what might be the results?
4. How many non-ideational uses of language might there be?

Science and idealism (§§54–81)
Summary
Mechanistic science had made such remarkable progress in the seventeenth century that Berkeley was aware that denying the reality of material substance seemed to offend successful scientific practice as much as it did common sense. Berkeley replies that his system threatens neither common sense nor science, if both these domains are properly understood. The business of science is not to offer metaphysical explanation but to state observed regularities in nature as clearly and economically as possible. (This view of science as primarily for expressing phenomena in mathematical laws was essentially that of Isaac Newton.) Thus, idealism and immaterialism are not only compatible with common sense and correct scientific practice, but they can actually help remove doubtful and ambiguous notions that have been serious blocks to understanding for common sense and science alike.

Section by section

§54 *Eighth objection*: Humanity collectively believes in matter and the existence of things external to the mind. Berkeley replies, first, that this belief may not be as close to universal acceptance as is alleged, and secondly, that a contradictory belief cannot be genuinely sustained. (Berkeley refers the reader to earlier remarks on the incoherence of material substance.) However, he does grant that people at least behave *as if* 'the immediate cause of their sensations . . . were some senseless unthinking being'. However, this kind of 'as if' behaviour does not offset or weaken the already-established point that no clear idea of material substance can be formed, and hence that no meaning or coherent philosophical doctrine ('settled speculative opinion') can really be annexed to 'material substance'.

But surely we can at least use the concept of material substance in grammatically correct utterances? For example, we might assert 'Material substance exists' and this doesn't sound like obvious nonsense. Berkeley would of course grant that we can use the words 'material substance' in conjunction, but this purely linguistic fact proves nothing about real possibility. Using a sentence does not imply that everything mentioned therein is truly possible. The phrase 'a five-sided rectangle' can feature in grammatically well-formed sentences (e.g. 'Brian proudly drew a five-sided rectangle on the board') but this does not prove such an object is possible. If Berkeley is correct, the idea of material substance is only *superficially* coherent; examined more closely, it proves to be an impossible combination of properties. Berkeley can grant that an existent which neither perceives nor yet is perceived doesn't seem obviously incoherent (as a five-sided rectangle presumably does), but then not all contradictory objects wear their incoherence in plain sight. (For a non-obviously, but genuinely, incoherent entity, consider an even prime number greater than two.)

§55 Further to the reply to objection 8: even *universal* assent is no guarantee of truth, especially when we remember how many ill-supported opinions and downright falsehoods have been believed by the 'unreflecting' part (i.e. the vast majority) of humanity. Even learned people at one time rejected the ideas of the Earth being in motion or possessing antipodes and these ideas still command little by way of widespread assent.

§56 *Ninth objection*: Further to objection 8, it strains credulity that we could all have made such a vast collective mistake in believing in matter when really there is no such thing and indeed, when the very concept of matter is actually incoherent. Why then have so many of us made this colossal mistake? Berkeley offers a psychological origin-story to account for the 'prejudice' in favour of matter and unperceived existence. People noted that they are presented with many different perceptual ideas. People also noted that such ideas very often don't depend on the exercise of their owners' imaginations for existence. Noticing that sensory ideas don't arise from the individual's will and show no signs of 'being excited from within', people attributed *independent* existence to the objects of perception themselves, 'without ever dreaming that a contradiction was involved in those words'. Philosophers saw part of the solution, which was to grasp that the objects of perception do not exist outside the mind. However, philosophers then made matters worse by adopting indirect realism about perception, whereby what we perceive directly is not the real objects themselves but their representations, and then arguing that the real objects in existence are mind-independent. Both the bulk of humanity and the philosophers made essentially the same mistake – having grasped that the causes of their ideas were external to, and independent of, their own minds, they made the fallacious assumption that they must be independent of all minds whatsoever. (A near-universal belief in a contradictory hypothesis is a strange thing. Berkeley's case might appear stronger if he could produce examples of other contradictory beliefs that were nonetheless embraced by most of humanity.)

§57 Why though do we reach for imperceptible substance to explain the generation and regularity of ideas not of our own making? Berkeley offers three reasons: (1) the total inertness of ideas and the contradiction in the very idea of imperceptible substance were not immediately apparent; (2) 'the supreme spirit which excites those ideas in our minds' is not presented to us as 'any particular finite collection of sensible ideas', in the way that human beings are presented to us through collections of sensible ideas of their limbs, faces, motion, etc.; and (3) God's purposes instead issue in regular and uniform sequences of sensible ideas (i.e. natural laws). We somehow feel that uniformity is not in need of any special explanation or invites an appeal to agency, whereas we are quick enough to infer supernatural agency when we see a miraculous interruption of the laws of nature. Erroneously, we take changefulness and variation in action to be the hallmarks of freedom, when really they are imperfections. So there is no contradiction in one and the same action being both law like and free – another rather Cartesian doctrine. Descartes upheld an essentially voluntarist view of belief and judgement, whereby judgement requires the combination of an idea proposed by the intellect with an act of the will (either an affirmation or a denial). In response to the objection that the clearest and most distinct beliefs seem to be those which are precisely *least* subject to our voluntary control, Descartes replies that freedom is not to be confused with arbitrariness or uncertainty – rather, the more clearly and distinctly I grasp an idea, the freer my affirmation of it is. (Cf. Descartes: 'We are also free – indeed at our freest – when a clear perception impels us to pursue some object', Cottingham, *Meditations*, Sixth Replies, 1986, p. 94.)

§58 *Tenth objection*: immaterialism seems inconsistent with received truths in both philosophy and mathematics. For example, science teaches us the Earth truly moves but yet the Earth's motion is not perceptible. Is immaterialism then opposed to heliocentrism? Berkeley replies that the hypothesis of the Earth's motion can (also) be explained in terms of what is perceptible. Accepting that the Earth moves is to accept, on the basis of astronomical observation, some statements about what we would perceive if placed in certain situations. Although not (yet) perceived, the Earth's motion is nonetheless *perceivable* and would be perceived in the right circumstances. So the 'moving Earth' hypothesis can still be made sense of in terms of possible, if not actual perceptions. (In other words, to accept that the Earth moves is to be prepared to assent to counterfactual conditions of the form: 'If I were taken into space and held motionless relative to the Sun, I would then see the Earth moving against the background of the stars'.) Later philosophers have paid a lot of attention to what might make such counterfactual conditionals true and many have concluded that empiricists, like Berkeley, have real difficulty in explaining how conditionals that make reference to unobserved but observable events can be true. The problem is that counterfactual conditionals are in a hypothetical mode and their antecedents (generally) refer to conditions that were never actualized. Without going into details here, the seas of language run a deal higher around counterfactual conditionals than early modern philosophy (and specifically Berkeley) thought.[46] In a nutshell, empiricists of Berkeley's stamp effectively have to make counterfactuals simply true or false, that is, resistant to further analysis, since counterfactuals by definition have false antecedents and non-existent states of affairs cannot be presented to perception. Such a view of counterfactuals is controversial. Michael Dummett, for instance, holds that a counterfactual conditional cannot be *simply* true; that is, if true, a counterfactual can only be true in virtue of some simple categorical statement, or in virtue of some statement that does not involve any (material or other form of) conditional. Cf. Dummett, 1993 (Loux (ed.), 2001, pp. 462–7).

§59 Knowledge of the regularities that nature exhibits allows us to make detailed plans for our future actions. Such knowledge allows us to predict not only what will happen to us but allows us to form considered judgements as to what would have happened to us had we been placed in different circumstances. (Note again the stress on possible, as well as actual, experience. It's an interesting question how actual perception licenses inferences to merely possible but unactualized perception.) This ability to derive counterfactual predictions about what our experiences would be like in different circumstances applies in all departments of the study of Nature, and is therefore applicable to astronomy and the movements of the planets too.

§60 *11th objection*: In this, and the sections immediately following, Berkeley considers a challenge from the (theist) materialist: If immaterialism is true, why should there be layers of microstructure in all physical objects? Why did God not simply install all correlations at the level of the immediately observable? (Why not clocks without clockwork?) Berkeley offers at least two replies here:

1. a '*tu quoque*' response, that is, that the demand for an explanation of microstructure is just as pressing for the materialist theist as it is for the immaterialist.

2. a 'natural language' response, that is, that Nature is a Divine Language with unlimited recombinative and expressive power (cf. *PHK* 65). The expressive power of the Divine Language is only increased by the addition of layers of structure and significance.

Science teaches us (particularly through the deliverances of microscopes) that there are hidden layers of detailed microstructure that underlie the sensible ideas we observe. Plants and animals alike show evidence of detailed organization at a level far below what we can apprehend with our unaided senses. What purpose can all this microstructure have if immaterialism is correct? Surely, it would have been within God's powers to have created, for example, all the sensible ideas of a growing tree without being obliged to create as well accompanying ideas of cell structure that are almost impossible to perceive ordinarily. If all causation is agency, properly conceived, then all the work that goes into making hidden internal structures seems so much effort wasted. Berkeley considers the example of a watchmaker: all the contrivance and skill that a watchmaker shows in fitting out the internal clockwork of the watch and ensuring that it runs smoothly seems needless if it's truly a spirit whose purposes create and regulate the motion of the watch. Why bother making it necessary for the watchmaker to exert all this effort? Indeed, why bother with microstructure at all? ('Why does not an empty case serve as well as another?') Likewise, why set up elaborate correspondences between the immediately observable properties of the watch and those of the microstructure? Why for instance does a breakdown in the working of the watch prove to be invariably correlated with some failure in the internal parts of the watch? Such questions can be asked not only of watches but of the whole system of nature. Can any explanation be given (in terms of 'final causes') why bodies show such intricacy of structure if this structure is scarcely if ever perceived?

§61 Berkeley replies to objection 11 in several ways: (1) he begins by supposing (clearly only for the sake of argument) that the 11th objection really was unanswerable. However, even if the 11th objection were unanswerable and microstructure was difficult, if not impossible, to explain on immaterialist lines, this would be only a small explanatory glitch to set against the *a priori* certainty of the incoherence and explanatory uselessness of matter. (As before, *a priori* demonstration trumps *a posteriori* argument. See also, for example, *PHK* §21.) (2) The need for an explanation for the existence of internal properties and microstructure is just as pressing, if not more pressing, for the (theist) materialist as it is for the immaterialist. For all philosophies, the question can be pressed of why God chose to effect His purposes through the complicated rigmarole of internal structures for plants and animals, rather than simply making the right sequences of events occur through a direct exertion of the Divine will, without any intermediaries. Indeed, this objection may be even *more* pressing for the materialist, given that Berkeley believes that he has already established the complete causal impotence of qualities like extension, figure and motion. Such qualities are (he thinks) merely ideas, and ideas can have no causal efficacy of their own, so materialists are in even worse straits than immaterialists once they try attempting to explain the existence of microstructure by invoking 'the existence of those machines without the mind'. (Berkeley refers the reader at this point to §25.) Again, the supposition of unperceived existence would be (even if coherent) of no explanatory use, since no one can explain how imperceptible objects manage to generate perceivable ideas.

§62 A further reply to objection 11 (and one Berkeley seems to hold in higher esteem than the two replies in §61): it may be that the creation of microstructure is not *absolutely* necessary for God's purposes (not least because God's omnipotence doesn't need any intermediary causes or instruments). However, microstructure may still be *useful* for God's purposes. In particular, microstructure may be uniquely useful for ensuring that Nature unfolds in an orderly, regular and predictable way. Berkeley originally espoused a less plausible view of microscopy and was less charitable about microstructure that we couldn't (directly) perceive. Originally, Berkeley seems to have held that the view down the microscope takes us quite literally into 'a new world: it presents us with a new science of visible objects quite different from what we behold with the naked eye,' (*NTV* 85). Microscopes produce ideas in us which lack the normal relationships to our tactile sensations and consequently, visual ideas obtained through a microscope are no part of the Divine Language, because they are not systematically correlated with tactile sensations. This would seem to commit Berkeley to holding that the use of microscopes thus adds nothing to our understanding of the world. The *PHK* view is much more plausible. The two views seem later to have been brought into resolution: the objects of microscopy are different from the objects we see with the naked eye, but then again the objects we see are different from the objects we touch – in all cases, there may be useful associations of ideas for us to learn (see *D* 245).[47] In short, the postulation of microstructure is of great use in helping us to formulate general laws and to regulate our expectations of how Nature will behave accordingly.

Learning the general rules that govern Nature is also of immense help to us in our attempts at creating artificial machines and new phenomena. For Berkeley, explanation *is* uncovering the general laws that govern phenomena. (This view of explanation was first sketched at §31, but both this view and its accompanying philosophy of science are returned to later on, in those sections of *PHK* on the methods of science, for example, §117.) Thus, while God ('the intelligence which sustains and rules the ordinary course of things') could directly (miraculously) cause all motions of a watch's hands without creating any internal workings for that watch, it may be that the regular course of Nature would be better served by allowing the watch to come into existence through the law-governed actions of a watchmaker and thereafter to run normally, with any interruptions of proper working accompanying breakdowns in the internal structure of the watch. So, while microstructure may not be essential for God's purposes, it can nonetheless be useful. God's creativity might even seem to be greater for having produced a world of many intricate layers of symbolic representation and discovery, and not just one, directly observable, layer. One might add that the existence of layers of microstructure might be an incentive to us to improve our instruments and understanding. Cf. Robert Hooke (1635–1703) on the possibility of creating artificial instruments to enhance our tactile sensitivity to match the enhanced visual acuity that microscopes permit: ''Tis not improbable also, but that the sense of *feeling* may be greatly improved, for that being a sense that judges of the more gross and robust motions of the Particles of Bodies, seems capable of being improv'd and assisted very many wayes.'[48]

§63 With the above said, Berkeley also allows that for certain purposes, God might find it useful to effect a more direct intervention into the state of the world and cause 'some appearance out of the ordinary series of things'. (Berkeley doesn't cite any cases here but such miraculous interventions might be made, for example, to give Divine endorsement to a particular figure or statement.) Although such interventions can be awe-inspiring and can help direct people's thoughts to God, the very need for regularity and predictability in Nature means that such interventions can only be made sparingly. In any event, many orthodox theists held that the better testimony to God's existence is found in the regularity of natural laws and not in their interruption.

§64 Berkeley now restates the original objection (no. 11) from §60: ideas do not arise at random but are produced in regular ways. Furthermore, some ideas are observed to occur together in regular combinations, 'like so many instruments in the hand of Nature', that seem to work secretly to produce the appearances we observe. But as ideas are causally quite inert, why are they only observed in combinations? Likewise, given that such combinations of ideas are not necessary for God's producing the effects He desires, what then are they for? Has God installed 'all that art and regularity to no purpose'?

§65 Berkeley replies to the above restatement of objection 11 in two ways: (1) He distinguishes between the pairs 'cause'/'effect' and 'sign'/'signified'. Ideas (singly or in combination) cannot possibly act as causes but they can act as signs. Thus, the characteristic colour of flame is *not* the cause of the burning I will feel if I bring my finger into close proximity with the flame; rather, the visual flame is a *sign* of the tactile sensation I will feel (i.e. burning) if I bring my finger any closer to the object I perceive. The (visual) idea of flame does not cause the (tactile) idea of burning but it does forewarn any observer of the impending tactile sensation. Thus, the flame stands to being burnt, not as cause to effect but as sign does to signified. (Note that Berkeley does allow we can observe genuine causation too. Suppose I form the intention to raise my arm and my arm is duly raised. Although I cannot observe my mind or its workings directly, nonetheless if my forming the intention (or volition) to raise my arm is succeeded by (visual and tactile sensations of) my arm rising, the volition does stand to the arm-raising as cause to effect, and not merely as sign to thing signified.) (2) He compares the forming of ideas into combinations with the forming of letters into words. In both cases, a limited number of components have their expressive power multiplied by being (capable of being) combined into many different arrangements. Furthermore, to keep these combinations of components both regular and of wide (even universal) significance, the combinations of components must be regulated by laws and intelligently maintained. (This notion of Nature as a gigantic Divinely maintained language is of the utmost importance in Berkeley's later works, such as *Alciphron*,[49] but can also be found in earlier works. Consider *NTV* 147: 'The proper objects of vision constitute an universal language of the Author of Nature, whereby we are instructed how to regulate our actions in order to attain those things that are necessary to the preservation and well-being of our bodies, as also to avoid whatever may be hurtful and destructive of them.' This 'Divine language' view of Nature also informs Berkeley's philosophy of science, whereby science aims to uncover the grammatical rules of the language of nature.) Thus, the real reason why ideas are found associated in combinations is to afford the greatest expressive power combined with the greatest economy of means and regularity of laws.

§66 Thus, many attempted explanations, wherein ideas or perceptible qualities figure as causes, run into absurdities. However, these absurdities disappear once we realize that what we took for causes are actually signs. Hence the proper aim of the 'natural philosopher' (or physical scientist) is not to try to offer causal explanations using perceptible qualities (as if any inert idea like extension or solidity could function as a cause) but rather to try and express as economically and generally as possible the links between those ideas that function as signs and those ideas that are signified thereby.

§67 *12th objection*: suppose we grant the impossibility of any sensible qualities existing in matter and we therefore reject the idea of an 'inert, senseless, extended, solid, figured, moveable substance', there remains the possibility that matter may exist as an inert, imperceptible substance that serves as an occasional cause whereby God is prompted to cause in us the requisite ideas of sense. Berkeley is keenly opposed to the existence of even such a stripped-down, negatively conceived notion of matter, for two reasons. First, the above conception of an inert, imperceptible substance is effectively that of a substance without any attributes, and Berkeley finds the idea of an attribute-free substance as incomprehensible as that of attributes surviving without a substance to inhere in. This alleged substance then is not distinguishable by its possession of any properties. (Other philosophers have taken both of these possibilities seriously however. Many metaphysicians have believed that all the qualities that concrete objects possess must reside in a substantial bearer that is distinct from all qualities – a 'bare particular' that somehow underlies and supports, without being identical with, the particular's qualities. Berkeley has much to say against such notions of quality-free substance. Alternatively, Hume's account of the self as a bundle of ideas or perceptions comes very close to the doctrine of attributes without a substantial bearer, as though the self truly were like Lewis Carroll's grin without a cat. However, no mere collection of ideas could think, on Berkeley's *PHK* system. Any collection of passive ideas would itself be a passive being.) However, unlike Locke (cf. *Essay* II/xiii/19), Berkeley is not sceptical about the notion of substance in general – mental qualities must exist in a mental substance after all – but rather confines his scepticism to specifically material substance. Secondly, the status and location of any such imperceptible, inert substance would be highly doubtful. We have established that it doesn't exist in the mind. Likewise, it cannot exist in any extra-mental place, as place implies extension and we have already seen that extension must exist only in the mind. Berkeley therefore concludes that this alleged substance could exist 'nowhere at all'. (As Berkeley's later remarks at §98 about time as the succession of ideas make clear, a non-mental substance couldn't even exist in time either. So then we are seemingly left with the conclusion that matter cannot exist in space or time, cannot exist inside the mind and cannot exist outside the mind either.)

§68 So what does all the above retrenchment by the materialist leave us with? The 'matter' we are now being asked to imagine is a thin and elusive thing. By now, Berkeley's imagined materialist opponent has been induced to surrender the mind-independence of such eminently material-seeming qualities as extension, solidity, number and motion, and accept that all such qualities must reside in mental substance. Thus far, the definition of 'matter' is all composed of negatives – that is, matter isn't extended or solid or capable of motion . . . etc. What positive conception can be invoked to stop the definition of matter becoming that of something purely negative? There seems little left to distinguish the above definition of matter from that of a complete non-entity, as though the concept of matter has been so pared down as to leave the word 'matter' a mere synonym for nothingness. The sole surviving positive character seemingly left for matter is the 'relative notion' of being a substratum or support of those qualities we perceive. But, as noted above in §§16–17, Berkeley thinks there is no sustainable notion of support whereby an imperceptible substance could support sensible qualities in the way that columns can support a roof. (Believing in such a relation would require our being able to form sensible ideas of the relata involved. However, where we can form sensible ideas of the columns that support a roof and the roof that those columns support, by definition we can form no ideas of the imperceptible substratum that supposedly lies beneath all our sensible ideas. Worse still for the materialist, Berkeley maintains that while relations are not themselves ideas, all relations are nonetheless entirely mind-dependent in any case. See §89.)

With the notion that matter is a substratum, a non-sensible something that somehow contrives to support sensible qualities, having been thoroughly pummelled Berkeley then imagines the materialist's last stand might be the notion of matter as an 'occasional cause' of our ideas. Assuming that matter as a substantial support of qualities has to be rejected, the materialist might now try to define matter as a mind-independent substance that serves as the occasional cause of our ideas. The notion of 'occasional cause' was common in medieval and early modern (seventeenth and eighteenth century) philosophy, and very prominent in the work of Malebranche, but is now rather far gone into disuse. Generally, an 'occasional cause' is not a necessitating event that brings its associated effect into being through its own direct power or influence. Rather, the occurrence of an 'occasional cause' serves as a sort of signal (or warning) of the occurrence of its associated effect, 'at the presence whereof God is pleased to excite ideas in us'. However, Berkeley maintains that this conception of matter won't do either. The notion of presence invoked here must be entirely metaphorical (if not downright incomprehensible), because no meaning can be given to the notion of an imperceptible substance being presented to consciousness.

§69 Berkeley then subjects the notion of 'occasion' to scrutiny. He distinguishes two senses in which something might be said to be an 'occasion'. First, the occasion of an effect might be the agent that produces that effect. Secondly, an occasion might be an event that precedes an effect, and is observed to accompany that effect. (An occasional cause in this second sense is close to what Hume would define as a cause *simpliciter*, for example, 'We may define a cause to be *an object, followed by another, and where all the objects similar to the first are followed by objects similar to the second*' (*Enquiry* 7/2, original emphasis).) However, neither sense of 'occasion' will help the materialist. No inert, passive thing can be an agent and wield genuine causal powers, so the first sense won't do. However, matter can't be an occasional cause in the second sense (that of being an observed accompaniment of an effect) either. If matter cannot be observed, it cannot (*a fortiori*) be observed to accompany anything else. Therefore we can attach no sense to the notion of matter being an occasional cause.

§70 Very well, the materialist might say, even granting that matter is not perceived by us and cannot be an occasional cause for us, it might still be perceived by God and used by God as 'an occasion of exciting ideas in our minds'. We can observe regularity in the way our ideas of sensation are produced, and this regularity suggests a like regularity in the occasions whereby our ideas are generated. So matter might still have a role in God's economy of Nature even if we can't perceive it. There might be 'certain permanent and distinct parcels of matter' which correspond to our ideas but are only perceived by God, and provide occasions for God to produce our ideas in a regular fashion.

§71 Berkeley notes that the conception of matter sketched in §70 is no longer that of a substance that can exist independently of all perception. However, in effectively asking him to reply to the possibility sketched in §70, the imagined materialist asks too much. After all, it isn't part of Berkeley's purpose, nor does he claim to be able, to give his readers a full inventory of the kinds of ideas that may be in God's mind. So, while Berkeley cannot possibly claim to have refuted the idea that God might keep certain ideas in His mind to act as occasions for producing our ideas (much as 'a musician is directed by the notes of music to produce that harmonious train and composition of sound, which is called a tune'), likewise this conception is not one that he need refute. This is partly because such a bizarre conception doesn't need a lot of refutation, since it presumably won't make much claim on our imagination anyway. However, mainly Berkeley doesn't need to respond in detail to this possibility because it concedes an awful lot to the immaterialist – the archetypes in God's mind postulated in §70 exist only by being perceived. Calling such Divine archetypal ideas 'matter' does nothing to make them more material in the sense Berkeley found objectionable, that is, existing independently of perception. In other words, the supposedly 'materialist' possibility sketched in §70 is indistinguishable from an immaterialist doctrine. The crucial concession has therefore been made and the materialist has been forced to give up the very mind-independence of existence that was the original defining characteristic of matter. Note that Berkeley is *not* denying here that there are ideas in God's mind nor that such Divine ideas might be identical with physical objects. Rather, he is denying that there are ideas in God's mind of some utterly unknown kind but which yet direct or guide God's activities. (See Ayers' edition of Berkeley's *Philosophical Works*, 1975, p. 99, fn. 1.)

§72 Reasoning will reveal to us that the uniform succession of our ideas of sensation invites explanation by reference to a wise and good agent. Beyond that, reasoning can't tell us very much. That this Divine Agent is infinitely powerful, wise and good is certainly a sufficient explanation for the regularities we perceive in Nature. Berkeley's argument here might look like an example of what modern philosophers call an 'inference to the best explanation', that is, an inference to the probable truth of whichever explanation best explains the phenomena of interest.[50] However, 'best' in this context usually involves some notion of ontological economy, obeying Ockham's Razor in other words, and postulating no more power or attributes in the object inferred to than are required for explanatory purposes. Berkeley doesn't seem to claim that omnipotence, omniscience and omnibenevolence are *demanded* by the facts or are the sole explanation that the facts will support; merely that they are more than sufficient to explain the facts. Perhaps Berkeley transgresses against Ockhamist ontological economy here. Perhaps he multiplies entities beyond necessity in thus inferring an infinitely powerful, wise and good God from appearances that are suggestive of great but perhaps only finite power, wisdom and goodness. (Certainly, Hume might press such an argument against Berkeley, that is, that Berkeley's premises at most support a deistic inference to some sort of powerful supernatural agent, not to the fully fledged infinite attributes of a theistically conceived personal God.) However, nothing we perceive favours the existence of 'inert senseless matter' and Berkeley challenges any doubters to demonstrate how any natural phenomenon can be explained better using the materialist hypothesis than it can be explained on immaterialist principles. Indeed, he still challenges any reader to make a coherent conception of matter. Matter can't be an occasion for the exciting of ideas as far as we are concerned (i.e. because we can't perceive this alleged occasion) and the inadequacies of conceiving matter as an 'occasional cause' whereby God is moved to produce our ideas were thoroughly explored in the previous section.

§73 Berkeley now pauses to reflect on the motivations that led people to materialism, and in effect to offer a potted history of the materialist hypothesis, in the hope that the ebbing of belief in these distinct phases will produce by like degrees a reduction in belief in matter. First, people formed the idea that perceptible qualities like colour, motion, etc. really existed outside the mind, and therefore that they needed some substance to inhere in. (Not least because people could not conceive how such qualities could exist separately, that is, without any substantival support. Note that Berkeley doesn't seem to allow that qualities can exist without inhering in some substance. Again, no bundle theory for Berkeley in *PHK*.) Next, people having concluded that secondary qualities could have no mind-independent existence, they imagined this substratum contained only primary qualities, such as extension, figure and motion. (Oddly enough, Locke speculated that we postulate substance as much for psychological as explanatory reasons: 'Not imagining how these simple *Ideas* can subsist by themselves, we accustom our selves, to suppose some *Substratum*, wherein they do subsist, and from which they do result, which therefore we call *Substance*', *Essay* II/xxiii/1.) These primary qualities they still believed to be mind-independent and to require some supporting substratum. However, we (i.e. those of us who have followed Berkeley's arguments) are in a position to know better and to throw off this outmoded and exploded psychological/historical weakness for materialism. We know that such qualities (whether 'secondary' or 'primary') can exist only in a perceiving substratum, hence we have no reason to believe in matter. Indeed, we are in a position to know that no such thing as matter, if conceived as an 'unthinking substratum' which supports qualities in existence outside the mind, can be coherent or could even be a possible existent.

It's interesting that Berkeley offers an account of why people have been predisposed to materialism and reluctant to abandon it, which appeals to habit, projection and other non-cognitive traits. Such a 'non-cognitive' approach to one's philosophical opponents has proved useful to philosophers of very different views from Berkeley. For example, David Hume would later come along and offer an account of the origins and persistence of religious belief which was similarly non-cognitive, to some extent in his *Dialogues Concerning Natural Religion* but rather more so in his *Natural History of Religion*.[51] Likewise, Hume's account of the origins and persistence of testimony to the occurrence of miracles emphasizes non-cognitive factors like a love of marvels and the wish to appear as a messenger of the Divine, etc. (See Hume, 'Of Miracles', *Enquiry*, §10.)

§74 If then a belief in matter arose purely through the need to posit some substantial support for the qualities we perceive, and this need can be safely demonstrated to be a mistaken basis for materialism, one would expect then that anyone who had been apprized of Berkeley's arguments would straightway cease to be a materialist. However, it doesn't seem to be so. We seem to be irrationally attached to a 'prejudice . . . riveted so deeply in our thoughts' in favour of matter that we are inclined to cling onto preserving the mere *name* of matter even if that name ends up being annexed only to the vaguest and most abstract notions of 'being' or 'occasion'. (Likewise, Hume argued that extra-rational forces like prejudice and habit played an important part in maintaining religious belief in the face of rational argument against it. Of course, Berkeley would find this particular application of non-cognitivist explanation anathema.) By this stage, Berkeley seems confident that all philosophical challenges to immaterialism have been anticipated and met, and hence that no *reasoned* philosophical objections to immaterialism could be put forward. Indeed, while he does later (§§82–4) consider some theological objections to immaterialism, he seems to proceed henceforth as though further *philosophical* objections to immaterialism can only proceed from extra-rational factors like prejudice, misunderstanding or mental sloth. (If the subsequent three centuries of critical reactions to *PHK* are anything to go by, many readers have not been wholly convinced on this last point.) Berkeley again invites the reader to imagine what possible basis sense-experience could afford for the notion that our ideas proceed ultimately from an inert, unconscious, imperceptible occasion, rather than from the boundless agency of an intelligent, all-sufficient spirit. Likewise, perception can reveal no conceivable reason why God should be '*directed* by an inert occasion to excite ideas in our minds' (original emphasis).

§75 Alas, even after argument has done its utmost, a residual belief in matter might still remain. Berkeley finds this clinging to an outworn prejudice in favour of matter a remarkable fact about human thinking. He confesses himself baffled as to why anyone would choose to put 'a stupid thoughtless *something*' between the self and God. However, imagination seems to relinquish the notion of matter only very reluctantly and will try to retain the name even in the absence of any clear idea or notion of what the thing referred to might actually be. Hence a (last-ditch) attempt to salvage the name, if not the substance, of matter by describing it as 'certain *unknown ideas in the mind of God'*. This rather vague description is all that is left once the notion of matter as an occasional cause for God is brought in.

§76 Disputes over whether or not 'occasional' ideas exist in the mind of God and, if they do, whether or not they are to be *called* 'matter', Berkeley dismisses as fruitless. Whatever the name given to ideas in God's mind, such ideas would still be mind-dependent entities and would therefore not be matter in the sense that Berkeley finds objectionable. (After all, given that Berkeley believes that the annexation of words to meanings is entirely arbitrary, it isn't the *name* that we give a substance that matters but what qualities that substance is supposed to comprehend.) However, if the substantial support of our ideas is conceived as inert, imperceptible and unthinking, then Berkeley rejects such a conception as involving a 'plain repugnancy'. Imperceptible substratum, by any other name, is still impossible.

§77 Suppose though that some new sense could exist, which might inform us of the properties of matter, although we can't possibly conceive of what the deliverances of this hypothetical sense might be like. (Any more than someone who is congenitally blind and has thus lacked visual ideas since birth could form a mental image of a colour.) Such a new sense might make the properties of matter as familiar and comprehensible to us as, for example, sight makes the ideas of light and colour to those of us who can see. Berkeley replies first that if matter is simply to be 'the unknown support of unknown qualities', then its existence and properties can't be any concern of ours, and any disputes about its properties would be essentially empty verbal disputes.

§78 A second, more searching, reply to the 'new sense' hypothesis follows: the senses can only work by furnishing us with ideas or sensations. (Sight gives us visual ideas of light and colour, touch gives us tactile ideas of texture and hardness.) All that a hypothetical extra sense could do would be to furnish us with more sensible ideas, albeit of a novel kind. We've already established that all ideas, howsoever generated or conveyed to us, must exist in the mind. Therefore, even if we possessed a new sense that gave us ideas of 'matter', these ideas could not inhere in, or in any way resemble, an imperceptible substratum. So a new sense would not affect Berkeley's conclusions one iota. In other words, the mind-dependence of the ideas of sense applies to all possible ideas of sensation, as well as all actual ones. (Again, the important claim is that mind-dependence is a conceptual discovery, not an empirical one. If we attend to the concepts of existence and perception, we can discover without further reflection that they are inextricably intertwined. Finding out that *esse* is *percipi* is thus more like discovering that no even prime number can be greater than two than it is like discovering that all metals expand when heated. Again, the *a priori* objection to the very coherence of material substance completely swamps any *a posteriori* disadvantages in immaterialism.)

§79 Another riposte from the materialist: granted no ideas can be formed of matter, matter has no explanatory function and matter cannot be conceived, yet it still doesn't seem contradictory to assert that a general substance could exist and be the occasion of our ideas, even if we can't put any clear meaning or annexe any positive ideas to the concept of matter. Berkeley replies that 'when words are used without a meaning, you may put them together as you please, without danger of running into a contradiction'. You can assert that '2 + 2 = 7' without falling into contradiction, provided you don't give these terms their usual meaning. Likewise, you can talk of an 'inert thoughtless substance without accidents' provided you don't mean what we normally mean by such a combination of terms. In other words, the above-sketched conception of matter is so threadbare that it possesses insufficient content to be contradictory. Where ideas cannot be formed, no 'repugnancy' can be demonstrated. (Cf. Philonous at *D* 225: 'You are not therefore to expect I should prove a repugnancy between ideas where there are no ideas; or the impossibility of matter taken in an *unknown* sense, that is no sense at all'.)

§80 A last-ditch materialist reply: matter might still exist as an unknown *something*, which doesn't fit our ordinary categories and can only be defined negatively. (Thus, it's 'neither substance nor accident, spirit nor idea' and is without causal powers, consciousness, extension or the possibility of motion). Berkeley takes a short way with this negative characterization of matter: the alleged *something* above characterized is indistinguishable from *nothing*, and makes the same impression on his mind.

§81 Further to the 'unknown something' definition above: the materialist might reply that the above definition is not purely or entirely negative – after all, it does at least include the positive conception of entity or existence. Berkeley replies that the idea of existence abstracted from perception is an entirely illegitimate abstraction, and such 'existence' is the most obscure abstract idea of them all. Berkeley offers an interesting sidelight here on possibilities for other kinds of spirits: he willingly grants that God has seen fit to create many other kinds of spiritual beings whose powers far exceed those of Berkeley himself. Berkeley allows that it would be 'the utmost folly and presumption' for him to legislate for the powers of conception of such beings, based on his own imaginative faculties. Angelic (or other spiritual) beings may be able to entertain ideas derived from senses of a kind quite unknown to us; ideas that are as different from anything we can perceive 'as colours are from sounds'. We cannot possibly imagine what ideas acquired through such unknown senses would be like. (Cf. 'And had Mankind been made with but four Senses, the Qualities then, which are the Object of the Fifth Sense, had been as far from our Notice, Imagination and Conception, as now any *belonging to a Sixth, Seventh or Eighth Sense*, can possibly be,' *Essay* II/ii/3.) However, it is not presumption on Berkeley's part to claim that no mind (however exalted in power) can entertain an idea that contains a manifest repugnancy. With this observation, Berkeley concludes his survey of philosophical objections to immaterialism and all that can be said on behalf of materialism.

Questions
1. What is the correct way to characterize matter and is Berkeley correct to focus on the notion of mind-independent existence?
2. Berkeley's notion of support seems somehow overly literal minded. Can we flesh out the notion of 'support' or 'substratum' in such a way as to defuse some of Berkeley's criticisms?
3. Does Berkeley succeed in establishing that ideas could not exist without a substance to inhere in? Granted that

Berkeley's is not a 'bundle' theory of the self, ought it to have been?

4. Supposing we grant Berkeley's objections to matter as an 'occasional cause' that God makes use of – could not a similar ('*tu quoque*') objection be urged against the idealist's reading of the elaborate conjunctions of signs we observe in Nature as a kind of language? After all, human beings use language as an instrument but then our finitude obliges us to use instruments – why does God speak to us only indirectly (via the natural world) and not directly?

ADVANTAGES OF IMMATERIALISM: PHILOSOPHY, SCIENCE, MATHEMATICS AND RELIGION (§§82–156)
Religious objections to immaterialism and replies (§§82–4)
Summary
In this short three-section segment of *PHK*, Berkeley considers (surprisingly briefly) some possible religious objections to immaterialism.

Section by section
§82 First, there are abundant Scriptural references to material things – including trees, cities and human bodies, among others. Berkeley simply repeats his earlier remarks that no genuine existent is imperilled by immaterialism, that he has already explained that bodies and corporeal objects are perfectly admissible in his system and that he has already explained how immaterialism maintains a principled distinction between '*realities*' and '*chimeras*' (citing §§29, 30, 33, 36, etc.). Berkeley concludes that nothing in Scripture is threatened by his doctrine and points out that there are no Scriptural references to 'matter' (in its philosophical acceptation – that is, as an inert, imperceptible substratum).

§83 Furthermore, we are all agreed that the correct use of language is confined to 'marking our conceptions, or things only as they are known and perceived by us'. Nothing in immaterialism threatens the correct use of language and this point has already been insisted upon sufficiently.

§84 A final religious objection: immaterialism makes miraculous interventions in the natural order less remarkable. It seems to diminish the miraculous transformation (in Exodus 7) of Moses' rod into a serpent to say that ideas of a rod were merely succeeded by ideas of a serpent in the minds of onlookers. Likewise, the miraculous transformation of water into wine at the marriage feast in Cana (John 2) seems diminished to mere conjuring if all Christ did was to impose wine-like sensory ideas (in place of water-like sensory ideas) on the marriage guests. The charge then is that immaterialism downgrades all Scriptural miracles to 'so many cheats, or illusions of fancy'. Berkeley replies by referring once again to his immaterialist criterion for distinguishing real existents from illusions. If the wedding guests at Cana found that *all* their sensory ideas of water had been replaced by sensory ideas of wine (including ideas of sight, smell, taste and the subsequent effects of consuming the wine) then the water *in itself* (i.e. in its essence) really became wine. So, Berkeley concludes, the appeal to 'real miracles' actually strengthens immaterialism rather than weakens it.

Questions

1. Does the Berkeleyan idealist have room for a principled distinction between genuine miracle-working and merely imposing on the senses of observers?
2. If someone could impose on all the senses of all observers simultaneously and give them a new but coherent set of sensory appearances, would there be any real sense in which the experiences thus generated could be described as false? Could Berkeley describe such 'commanded' experiences as delusory, and, if so, how?

Further advantages of immaterialism (§§85–100)

Summary

Materialism has prevented the understanding of the doctrine of bodily resurrection. Remove matter from the equation and perplexities about resurrection disappear. The insistence on the separate existence of matter has given comfort to sceptics of all persuasions since the dawn of ancient philosophy and has provoked endless religious controversies, for example, over the Resurrection and the apparent co-eternity of God and matter. At *PHK* 97, Berkeley again reviews his reasons for rejecting abstract ideas. At *PHK* 98, he analyses the nature of time and argues that mental substance must always involve the activity of cogitation.

Section by section

§85 Having canvassed, and replied to, all the philosophical and religious objections to immaterialism that he could invent, Berkeley turns to the more positive task of elucidating the philosophical advantages of immaterialism. The chief general advantage is that of relieving philosophy from obscure notions and inconclusive verbal squabbles. A host of hitherto intractable philosophical questions vanish once immaterialism is accepted. Examples are many but include the following:

- The long disputes over the infinite divisibility of matter disappear if no material substance exists to be divided. (As we shall see at §141, Berkeley accepts the Cartesian idea that mind is essentially indivisible so no parallel problem about whether or not mind is infinitely divisible arises for immaterialists.)
- Philosophers long wondered whether or not material substance could think, and many confessed themselves unable to conceive how an essentially extended substance could have the power of thought. For example, Locke concluded that on balance God could have annexed the power of thought to matter but in fact probably hadn't done so. So, while Locke thought that the balance of probabilities favoured substance dualism, he seems to have thought that materialist monism was at least a coherent possibility and that thinking matter was only *contingently* (as opposed to absolutely or logically) impossible. Berkeley of course would not accept any of this – holding instead that material substance was a necessary and not contingent impossibility. For Locke, thinking matter may not exist but it could have existed, had God willed differently; for Berkeley, thinking matter cannot exist because *a fortiori* matter cannot exist and there are no conceivable circumstances in which this impossibility could have been different.
- Likewise, the problem of mind/body interaction disappears if only mental substance exists. (Admittedly, mind/body

interaction disappears if only matter exists but of course Berkeley would find materialist monism incoherent.)

Besides the above, there are other advantages in imma-terialism for religion and science, which Berkeley treats of in subsequent sections.

§86 From this section until roughly §134, Berkeley considers advantages to our understanding of ideas, covering general advantages in §§86–100 and particular advantages in §§101–32, with §§133–4 summarizing the advantages considered thus far.

In the light of the previous discussion, Berkeley now divides human knowledge into two areas, namely knowledge of ideas and knowledge of spirits. Taking 'ideas *or unthinking things*' (emphasis added) first: a great cause of philosophical confusion has been the belief that ideas can exist in two ways. Philosophers have erred in contrasting the 'intelligible' existence of ideas within the mind with their 'real' existence outside the mind. This has encouraged the belief that unthinking things can have an absolute existence, quite apart from their being perceived. This in turn has led to scepticism. People held that knowledge was possible only in so far as it related to real things, and real things in turn were those that existed outside the mind. Combine these views with a representative theory of perception, whereby we are not directly acquainted with the real objects of our per-ceptions, and scepticism seems inevitable. The above doctrines immediately invite the question of how we can possibly know that our ideas are adequate to the real objects that cause them if real objects are forever beyond our perceptual grasp.

§87 If we consider qualities like colour, figure, motion, etc. as they present themselves to our minds via our senses, we find nothing mysterious about them. Such qualities (considered as sensory ideas) are perfectly transparent to our perception and hence to our understanding. However, once we start treating these ideas as mere effects of some other, hidden qualities that somehow signify '*things* or *archetypes* existing without the mind' then scepticism follows. Again, the 'representationalist' problem arises of how we can know that there is any similarity between our familiar sensory ideas and their hypothetical imperceptible causes. We know qualities only in so far as, and in the ways in which, they register on our senses. (Remember Berkeley's

'Likeness Principle' that representation requires resemblance, and ideas can only resemble other ideas.) If we admit another mode of existence for these qualities, their causes or archetypes then of that other existence, we can't form any understanding whatsoever. Indeed, our sensory ideas may totally fail to correspond with their real causes. All such sceptical consequences follow from distinguishing the existence of things from that of ideas, and holding that things exist without the mind. (Berkeley also notes the historical popularity of arguments like the above with sceptics, whose arguments often if not invariably trade on the difference between the *external* existence of *things* and the *internal* existence of *ideas*.)

§88 Again, if we accept the possibility that things can exist unperceived (or without any reference to perception), then we allow the possibility that we may be mistaken not only with respect to the properties of real things but even over their very existence. Philosophers have been forced into universal distrust of their senses, extending even to suspecting the existence of their own bodies, as a result of these principles. All this can be avoided if we simply join Berkeley in rejecting the idea that terms like 'absolute', 'external' or 'exist' can have any meaning independently of perception. Berkeley reiterates that the existence of perceived objects is no easier a thing for him to doubt than is his own existence. It's flatly contradictory, on Berkeley's principles, to assert that an object should be 'immediately perceived by sight or touch' and yet not exist.

§89 Philosophical investigations using terms like 'being' or 'existence' must remain profitless until we are clear what these terms mean. According to Berkeley, 'thing' or 'being' can mean only two kinds of entities: spirits and ideas. It's perhaps unfortunate that we use the same terms (i.e. 'thing' and 'being') indifferently to denote two such radically different kinds of entity. Spirits and ideas are totally heterogeneous entities – the former active, indivisible and substantial; the latter inert, fleeting and dependent. Ideas cannot exist on their own but must be supported by a mental substance or spirit. We know our own minds by 'inward feeling or reflection' but we know other minds only through reasoning and inference. (This last is itself quite a concession to scepticism, since it risks making knowledge of other minds merely analogical or otherwise indirect.)

We can form at least notions of the workings of active spirits but strictly we can form no ideas of such beings. Likewise, we can form *notions* of the relations between spirits and ideas, although we cannot form ideas of such relations.[52] Berkeley further specifies that such relations are not themselves ideas, not least because we can perceive the things related without perceiving the relations between them. So, really there are three possible objects of human knowledge: ideas, spirits and relations. (Strictly speaking, the word 'idea' should not be applied to the last two categories.)

Alas, Berkeley's radical particularism about relations won't do. As with Locke's account of abstract ideas, questions recur, like:

- In virtue of what do we judge that two particular ideas resemble one another?
- What is it for one idea to resemble another?

If a judgement of resemblance between particular ideas refers to another particular idea, then an infinite regress looms, but if the judgement refers to a shared property, we seem left with universals. Likewise, particularism about relations seems especially unappealing, seemingly implying that each instance of resemblance is itself a particular. Relations have a being different from sense-data and physical objects. If resemblances aren't brute facts, they require recurrent features of reality, that is, universals. It doesn't help to say that minds create relations like resemblance via volitions, for the question still arises of what it is the mind has thereby created and what allows the mind to perform this feat. Such problems led Bertrand Russell (1872–1970) to reject nominalism and Berkeley's particularism about relations, in favour of a new empiricism that allowed direct knowledge (by acquaintance) of universals.[53]

§90 Berkeley again specifies that sensory ideas are real things but cannot exist outside the mind nor resemble (or be caused by) some extra-mental archetype. What we perceive may be rightly called 'external' but only in the sense of being external to our minds. However, this is because our sensory ideas are generated by a spiritual being external to our particular minds, *not* because our sensory ideas can exist externally to all mind. So, sensible objects need not exist discontinuously: 'when

I shut my eyes, the things I saw may still exist, but it must be in another mind'.

§91 Nothing in immaterialism (properly understood) diminishes in any way the reality of the things that we perceive. Everyone agrees that sensible qualities (including all the so-called primary qualities like extension, figure, motion, etc.) must exist in some substance, such qualities being incapable of self-supporting, independent existence. Sensible qualities for Berkeley include both Lockean primary and secondary qualities (e.g. 'colour, figure, motion, smell, taste, etc.', *PHK* 7), and thus they run athwart the traditional primary/secondary divide. Immaterialism does not challenge the reality of sensible qualities or sensible objects. Immaterialism and materialism thus differ, not over the status of the things we perceive but over the manner of substance that supports them. With immaterialism, sensible qualities reside in mental substance, while materialism places sensible qualities in an inert substance that exists independently of perception.

§92 Just as materialism supports scepticism, so does it support atheism. The difficulty of conceiving how matter could be created out of nothing led 'the most celebrated among the ancient philosophers' (i.e. Aristotle, 384–322 BCE) to argue that matter was not created at all, but was an eternally existent thing, coeval with God.

§93 Further reasons why materialism has supported atheism: First, if the soul is only material, it must be divisible and hence subject to decay and mortality. Secondly, without immaterial spirit, we can make no sense of free will. Thirdly, rejecting immaterial substance removes all force from arguments that an intelligent designer created and sustained the world. (Here Berkeley's target is much closer to modern materialism, that is, the monistic doctrine according to which all that exists is material.) Instead of design, materialism sees only chance or physical necessity at work in the world.

§94 Idolatry likewise has been greatly assisted by materialism. If people realized that the objects they perceive are inextricably mind-dependent then they would not worship mere concatenations of their own ideas (like the Sun, the Moon or a humanly manufactured idol) but instead address their worship to God. (The use of 'their own' here presumably refers to ownership, not origins. My sensory ideas of the Moon are mine in the sense that they exist in my mind but they don't of course proceed from my mind. They may be owned by me but they certainly aren't invented by me.)

§95 Even when not espoused by atheists, materialism has still disastrously infected Christian thought. Materialism makes bodily resurrection harder to comprehend and offers support to sects like the Socinians who denied the resurrection and/or divinity of Jesus.[54] The difficulties Berkeley seemingly has in mind are those attendant on trying to understand how one and the same person could have a physical body (or organism) that ceased to exist at death and then (maybe after a very long interval) received another body. He maintains all such difficulties disappear once we realize they spring from materialist assumptions that the body's identity is somehow distinct from that of the ideas it arouses in us. However, if we reason like good immaterialists, we'll realize the identity of the body is simply a matter of the continuity of the sensible ideas it arouses.

§96 Matter once disposed of, a host of fruitless sceptical, philosophical and theological disputes will also vanish. Indeed, Berkeley says, even if the arguments against matter had not amounted to a disproof (*a priori*) of its existence, the (*a posteriori*) reduction in trifling disputes consequent on abandoning materialism would (just in itself) be a powerful argument for immaterialism. (However, we shouldn't push this '*a posteriori*' line too far. We could avoid philosophical problems about personal identity just by denying that there are any persons, and while this strategy has been seriously adopted,[55] it seems to cut the knot rather than untie it and, in any case, hasn't commanded wide assent.)

§97 Berkeley now returns to the other great source of philosophical error (i.e. besides the belief in existence external to perception), namely the doctrine of abstract (general) ideas. Things that are perfectly familiar taken in the concrete have a nasty habit of turning incomprehensible once they are considered in the abstract. Time, place and motion, for example, are perfectly familiar to our everyday understanding but become hedged about with formidable difficulties once subjected to metaphysical scrutiny. Arrange an appointment for a certain time and place, and your meaning will be perfectly understood, but try considering 'time' abstracted from all particular circumstances (e.g. of date or duration) and confusion sets in.[56]

§98 What then can we make of an idea of time? Well, the best Berkeley can seemingly do is to consider the 'succession of ideas in my mind, *which flows uniformly, and is participated by all beings*' (emphasis added). (Although we might wonder at this point how we could possibly know that other beings experience time at the same rate that we do.) Time simply cannot be abstracted from the succession of ideas in our minds – no more abstracted or 'metaphysical' conception is possible. (Contrast with this view with that of Locke, for example, at *Essay* II/i/9, who held that the succession of ideas is simply our *evidence* for the passage of time. Berkeley however seems to believe that time's passage is *constituted* by the succession of our ideas – another case where Berkeley takes a condition as constitutive which other philosophers might see as evidential.) To try to form any other idea of time is immediately to be 'lost and embrangled in inextricable difficulties'. In particular, the doctrine of time's infinite divisibility leads to confusing and conflicting notions – on the one hand, that the spirit can exist through vast reaches of time while being unaware or, on the other hand, that the spirit is destroyed and re-created every second. (It's not immediately clear why Berkeley thinks that infinite divisibility of time leads to these odd consequences. However, Berman (1994, pp. 63–5) offers some ingenious suggestions.) Therefore, the duration of a spirit must be measured in the number of ideas (or actions) that succeed one another in the spirit's consciousness. Thus, Berkeley says (in another Cartesian-sounding conclusion) that 'the soul always thinks'. To buttress this conclusion, he again appeals to the reader's cognitive powers: try abstracting a spirit's existence from that spirit's thinking and you'll find this yet another impossible abstraction.[57]

§99 Similarly, any attempt at considering extension and motion in abstraction will create incoherencies. In particular, attempts at forming abstract ideas of extension go awry in two ways: first, they try to remove extension from all other sensible qualities, and secondly, they try to abstract extension from perception. In fact, extension can only exist in combination with other sensible qualities and it can exist only through being perceived. Sensible objects are constituted only by such combinations of ideas.

§100 Even if they could be formed, abstract ideas are not necessary for our understanding. We all know what it is to be happy, without being able to abstract the idea of happiness 'from all particular pleasure'. Similarly with justice and virtue, we can identify instances of, and work happily with, both qualities without being able to form an abstract idea of either. Indeed, the view that we can, and ought to, form such abstract ideas of moral qualities has probably been an impediment to moral philosophy.

Questions

1. Is it the case that materialism and immaterialism differ over the substance in which perceived things subsist and not over the existence of perceived things?
2. If time is purely constituted by the succession of our ideas, does that then imply that each of us inhabits a unique personal time?
3. Does Berkeley make a good case for why materialism corrodes belief in free will and (hence) moral responsibility?
4. Could atheism survive the loss of material substance?
5. Must corpuscularian science have the sceptical consequences Berkeley claims?

'Two great provinces of speculative science' (§§101–7)

Summary

Berkeley now turns to consider in detail the two sciences which deal with the material furnished to the mind through the senses, namely natural philosophy and mathematics. His aim in natural philosophy is to oppose the apparent triumph of scepticism. Berkeley cites as evidence of the overthrow of common sense by sceptical attack, the doctrine of the distinction of real essence from what we perceive. He also questions the universal Newtonian appeal to forces of attraction. His aim in mathematics is to relieve it from the incoherent notions of infinite divisibility and abstract ideas. Overall, Berkeley thought Newtonian science fostered scepticism, atheism and materialism.[58]

At *PHK* 103, Berkeley takes as his example of an apparently mechanical but in actuality occult hypothesis that of attraction.

Berkeley allows that there is a range of phenomena for which attraction can be made to appear a sufficient explanation. However, Berkeley criticizes the uncritical use of attraction as a catch-all physical hypothesis by inviting the reader to imagine what is signified by this term. He duly finds the term as a means of rendering ideas inadequate, since it does nothing to denote the causal power by means of which these effects occur. Berkeley cautions against assuming that observed correlations are exceptionless or can be generalized universally (*PHK* 106). He thinks we accept too readily the uniformity of nature and lay too much stress on arguments by analogy.

Section by section

§101 Speculative science, in dealing with ideas and their relations, has 'two great provinces', namely natural philosophy and mathematics. (The former is roughly equivalent to physics but could equally be glossed as natural science. The natural sciences are covered in §§101–17, while mathematics is further subdivided, with §§118–22 covering arithmetic and §§123–32 covering geometry.) Physical science has seemingly done sceptics a great favour, by reinforcing the sceptical belief that we can know nothing of the real nature and essence of objects. Scientists often conclude that we can be directly aware of only the outward properties of objects, while remaining ignorant of their essences. The evidence of the senses is thus almost wilfully misleading, and the smallest particles of matter contain (so we are told) mysteries that we cannot fathom. However, these sceptical conclusions are misplaced, since immaterialism suggests that our senses are demonstrably trustworthy and reveal to us objects in their full reality.

§102 Part of the reason why such sceptical mistrust of the senses has proved popular is the belief that every object (sensible objects presumably included) 'includes within itself the cause of its properties'. (In other words, that objects have their observable characteristics in virtue of causal powers and qualities that are intrinsic to those objects.) This belief in inner essences has historically been combined with a belief in 'occult qualities' (i.e. qualities that are somehow explanatory but unobservable) or 'inner essences'. (Such 'occult' explanation was often charged to Aristotelian and Scholastic philosophers.)

However, recent and contemporary (i.e. corpuscularian) philosophy has increasingly made reference to mechanical causes, such as extension, solidity, motion, etc. However, whether the explanatory principles appealed to are occult or mechanical, both schools mistakenly treat matter as capable of being a repository of causal powers, whereas in fact the only true causation is agency. Hence appealing to qualities like figure, motion and solidity to explain why we observe the colours and sounds that we do is effort wasted. Such waste of effort is inevitable whenever we try to explain the occurrence of one idea by appealing to another idea as a cause. Mechanical qualities are no more illuminating or explanatory than Scholasticism's intrinsic affinities between bodies. Where Scholastic explanation used teleological explanations and held that fire sought to travel upwards because the overarching sphere of fire had the greatest affinity to it, corpuscular explanation reduced ideas to mechanical qualities (like attraction, cohesion and rigidity) of minute, imperceptible bodies. In both cases, the appearance of reduction is misleading and the pretended 'explanation' a failure. Natural science would be greatly assisted, and greater economy of effort achieved, if we could abandon explanation by efficient causation: 'I need not say, how many *hypotheses* and speculations are left out, and how much the study of Nature is abridged by this doctrine.' Far from urging a return to Scholasticism, Berkeley wishes to remove metaphysical explanations from science.

§103 Mechanical explanation using the notion of attraction (or 'The mutual drawing of bodies') is now in vogue. However, appealing to attraction as an explanatory principle gets us no closer to genuine explanation: 'Nothing is determined of the manner or action, and it may as truly (for aught we know) be termed *impulse* or *protrusion* as *attraction*.' The term 'attraction' signifies nothing substantive beyond the observed effect and any appearance of giving a deeper or more profound level of explanation is illusory. The same is true of Berkeley's secondary example, namely the use of 'cohesion' to explain the persisting structure of steel. Again, the reader is challenged to imagine what, if anything is signified by the substantive term beyond the observed effect. The conclusion remains that the invocation of mechanical terms only restates the observations of phenomena and 'as to the manner of the action whereby it is produced, or the cause which produces it, these are not so much as aimed at'.

The mechanical and 'occult' metaphysical explanations peddled by corpuscularians and Scholastics should be replaced by explanations based on a familiar, cognizable example of causal power. We derive our notion of efficient causation from our experience of the operation of spirit, hence here is the correct model for causation. However, in pursuit of the utmost descriptive generality and economy, science may use terms which have no referent and which function only as devices to ease explanation. Scientists may use any algebraic devices in pursuing economical expression, provided they heed the chief of all metaphysical errors, that is, assuming that every substantival noun must name a real existent. Such is not the only function of language, which can also serve to excite the passions or place the mind in a 'particular disposition'. Again, a term need not be annexed to a single, determinate idea in order to be meaningful and useful (cf. *PHK*, Introduction §20).

§104 In modern parlance, Berkeley holds that explanation in the sciences consists in bringing the phenomenon to be explained under a covering law or regularity. This is the only sort of explanation that the physical sciences can offer. (Traditionally, opponents of such 'regularity' accounts of causation and natural laws maintain that such accounts mistake the evidence for a law of nature for the law itself.)

§105 Next, Berkeley offers an account of collecting observations in the method of the natural sciences, or what it is about collecting diverse observations that makes this symptomatic of the scientific enterprise. We must first recognize a similarity between the diverse phenomena to be collected. (This emphasis on scientists' collecting and selecting phenomena based on observed resemblances (or dissimilarities) is reminiscent of the scientific method recommended by Francis Bacon, in his *Novum Organum* (1620) and elsewhere.[59]) At least something, Berkeley thinks, might strike the eye as common between our observations of falling bodies, the movement of the tides and the phenomena of cohesion, that is, this common factor is 'an union or mutual approach of bodies'. The appearance of oddity in this collection is merely the product of the familiarity of some of the phenomena collected and the relative unfamiliarity of others. The perception of the natural scientist is exercised in precisely this matter of deciding which phenomena, although perhaps presenting an appearance to the contrary, in fact do exhibit the same general class of attributes. Thus, the difference between natural philosophers (or scientists) and untutored observers is not that the former have more incisive vision but rather that their vision encompasses more. The aim is not to penetrate to some barely accessible essence but rather to formulate rules of the broadest possible scope.[60]

§106 Berkeley held that we generalize compulsively; suffering that 'eagerness of the mind, whereby it is carried to extend its knowledge into general theorems' and that 'We should proceed warily in such things; for we are apt to lay too great a stress on analogies, and to the prejudice of truth.' Berkeley cautions his readers against our tendency to pass from observations of the bodies around us to conclusions about bodies in general. Berkeley stresses that generalization from experience is risky. He cautions against assuming that the correlations we observe must necessarily be exceptionless or can be generalized universally. Experience often suggests the opposite lesson. It is God's will that 'certain bodies' should 'cleave together' and God is equally capable of determining the attributes of bodies so they possess 'a quite contrary tendency to fly asunder'.

Thus, the voguish (Newtonian) hypothesis that every object tends to attract every other object should not be generalized recklessly. Berkeley cites in opposition to the doctrine of universal gravitation other observations which may tend to refute it. Berkeley's counter-examples to universal gravitation are (1) the failure of the fixed stars to show any tendency to approach one another as terrestrial objects do; and (2) the tendency of plants to grow against gravity (*PHK* 106). However, nowadays we don't see these phenomena as instances of 'a quite contrary principle', (ibid.) but rather as perfectly consistent with universal gravitational attraction. Still, Berkeley's caution about overgeneralizing remains after his unfortunate examples have fallen away. (Although Berkeley's notion of which phenomena are compatible with universal gravitation seemingly improved by 1713. At the close of the Third Dialogue, Philonous invites Hylas to consider how the water from a fountain will first rise and then fall back, 'its ascent, as well as descent, proceeding from the same uniform law or principle of *gravitation*' (*D* 263). This whole passage is a striking metaphor for how Berkeley believes training in philosophy will at first view seem to lead towards scepticism and away from common sense but proves ultimately the great restorative of common sense against scepticism.)

§107 There are four lessons to be drawn about the scope and methods of science. First, there is no way of arriving at efficient causes through the scientific investigation of phenomena. The motivation whereby God assigns properties to objects might remain forever inscrutable and is thus not a fit subject of scientific enquiry. However, secondly, there is a positive aspect to this recognition of the Divine Will as the driving force of Nature, in that the contemplation of phenomena is the contemplation of God's works, and while speculating about final causes is likely to prove a hindrance to the scientist, 'it should seem to become philosophers'. The third point is that the study of the history of Nature has been in no way shown to be a profitless exercise by this exposition. The study of Nature can still give rise to instructive lessons even though any general conclusions that may be drawn are the result not of 'immutable habitudes, or relations between things themselves' but rather the outcome of the benign architecture of the world installed by God. The fourth lesson that Berkeley draws has again something in common with one of Newton's methodological principles, namely that we may discover general laws from our observations and 'from them deduce the other phenomena'. In his major contribution to natural religion, Berkeley offers a version of the Design (or teleological) argument for God's existence which supplements his earlier theistic arguments from the nature of existence and the continuity of perceived objects. In particular, Berkeley argues that the world shows unmistakeable hallmarks of 'the workmanship of a *wise and good agent*' (emphasis original), who can only be God.

Questions

1. Does Berkeley's account of explanation by means of regularities anticipate Hume's account of causation? Are such regularity accounts plausible?

2. Is agency the best, or the only, model of causation we have available? Is agent causation any more intelligible than material causation?

3. Does Berkeley's insistence on the calculating, and not the representative, aspects of science make him into a species of positivist?

The attack on absolute space (§§108–17)

Summary

Again Berkeley cautions against taking analogies too far; in this case the error to be avoided is taking too focused an interest in grammatical rules for manipulation of signs and thereby neglecting the signs themselves, or what they stand for. Following on from his definition of the limits of experimental science, Berkeley discusses a particular example of the failure to observe such strictures. This is the case of Newtonian absolute space, which is supposedly an eternal, uniform substantival space which is yet imperceptible to any of our senses. Berkeley rejects absolute space because anything which cannot be perceived cannot be part of the objects of experience, and hence would have no reason to exist. Furthermore (*PHK* 116–17): (1) no eternal, uncreated being can exist besides God, and (2) a space which is not visual or tactile, but somehow common to both, is incoherent.

Section by section

§108 Those scientists (and here Berkeley means Newton) who derive general laws from phenomena and then use the laws to predict new phenomena, reason only about 'signs rather than causes'. They use their derived laws as mere inference tickets for predicting and accommodating phenomena, and not to offer metaphysical explanations.[61] Throughout his published writings, Berkeley takes this as correct scientific practice. (Cf. *DM* 35: 'It is not, however, in fact the business of physics or mechanics to establish efficient causes, but only the rules of impulsions and attractions, and, in a word, the laws of motions, and from the established laws to assign the solution, not the efficient cause, of particular phenomena'.)

In viewing science as descriptive and not explanatory, Berkeley was (arguably) aligning himself with Newton's philosophy of science and anticipating modern scientific instrumentalism. Newton maintained that his aims were confined to calculating and predicting the movements of physical bodies and also famously refused to speculate as what mechanism might produce gravitation. (Hence Newton's slogan 'Hypotheses non fingo', or 'I frame no hypotheses'.[62]) Berkeley closes §108 by comparing those who overstrictly adhere to observed regularities in Nature and those who fall into bad writing through overscrupulous attention to merely grammatical rules.

§109 However, having distinguished scientific from metaphysical enquiry and insisted that the former has no business with the latter, Berkeley also warns that 'We should propose to ourselves nobler views' than merely formulating descriptive rules about physical phenomena without entertaining metaphysical speculation as to what may be responsible for the existence and maintenance of these rules. In other words, the business of philosophy has a more noble aim than that of natural science, since the latter, if managed properly, is debarred from considering the ultimate ends for which things are framed. Thus, Berkeley's strictures against final causes in physics were intended to prevent scientists from getting above themselves and tackling questions they have no warrant to investigate.

§110 Berkeley refers the reader to 'a celebrated treatise on mechanics' (i.e. Newton's *Principia*) as an exemplar of the correct way to conceive natural science. However, Berkeley also maintains that this treatise illustrates the unfortunate consequences that can follow when inquiries into final causes and the postulation of occult explanations take the place of correct scientific practice. That Newton's *Principia*, and Newtonian absolute space, are Berkeley's targets is made clear by the allusion to a work which divides space into absolute and relative. In part, Berkeley's case against Newtonian absolute space is that Newton failed to adhere to his own methodological principles and strayed into metaphysics.

§111 Berkeley thinks absolute time, that is, time abstracted from the succession of sensible ideas and applied to the 'perseverance of the existence of things', was disposed of in §§97–8. Absolute space, however, warrants lengthier treatment.

According to Newton, space can be regarded in two ways: as relative (e.g. the spaces we perceive) and as absolute. This latter space is the unchanging substance beneath our visual and tactual experiences; imperceptible, omnipresent and perfectly uniform. Absolutists (or *substantivalists*) about space believe space is an entity in its own right, part of the irreducible furniture of the world. *Relationalists* about space, on the other hand, think space is simply the (actual or possible) spatial relations between objects. Thus, for relationalists, space is not a thing in its own right, but depends upon objects for its existence. For an absolutist, space would still exist even if all physical objects disappeared. For a relationalist, removing all objects would also remove space. Berkeley (like Leibniz) upheld a relational view of space.

Crucially for Berkeley, Newton said absolute space is imperceptible and we can only perceive *relative* spaces – the movable measures of absolute space defined in terms of relations between objects. Newton defines 'absolute place' as that part of absolute space which a body occupies, so it too is imperceptible. So, as absolute space and place are imperceptible, we must make do with the moveable measures of relative space. (In practice, we usually treat the Earth as stationary and define motion relative to it.) Using relative spaces means one and the same body can be at rest or moving, depending on which body we take as reference point. Because of these shifting relative motions, Newton thought science should attend to absolute motions. Where absolutists allowed that objects can be moving with respect to space itself, relationalists can only define motions relative to physical bodies.

Slightly embarrassingly for Newton, uniform motion through absolute space was supposed undetectable. Just as a body can be in relative motion without being in absolute motion, objects can also be in absolute motion without being in relative motion. For example, if the whole physical universe moves through absolute space with uniform velocity, it would undergo absolute motion, without any physical object therein experiencing relative motion. (Cf. *PHK*, Dancy edition, Introduction, p. 19.) Since Newtonians thought space was uniform and continuous, the doctrine of absolute space unfortunately implied that the whole physical universe could have any one of an infinite number of velocities and yet no possible experiment could determine which value was correct.

However, while Newton admitted that absolute space and (uniform) absolute motions cannot be perceived, he also held that absolute *accelerations* can have perceptible effects. In particular, Newtonian absolutists about space claim that relationalists can't explain the observable effects of so-called recessionary forces.[63] To bolster this claim, Newton offered his 'bucket' argument for the reality of absolute space.

Newton's bucket argument (see Alexander, pp. 152–60) goes thus: imagine a bucket suspended from a twisted cord. Water is poured into the bucket. The bucket is released and undergoes angular acceleration as the cord unwinds. At the instant the bucket is released, the water surface is flat (because it hasn't had time to adjust to the bucket's rotation). At this instant, the bucket receives the greatest impetus from the cord and hence its motion relative to the water will be greatest. However, this period of greatest relative motion between water and bucket is accompanied by a flat water surface (i.e. no change). However, as the cord unwinds and the bucket's angular velocity increases, the water surface becomes (progressively more) concave as the water recedes away from the axis of rotation and rises up the sides of the bucket. The water recedes from the axis of rotation because inertia compels it towards the tangential straight-line path it would take if the vessel's walls weren't there. (Such effects are familiar in many contexts. If you're in a car that takes a sharp bend, you will feel a recessionary force apparently pushing you towards the outside edge of the turn. In fact, you're feeling a force generated by the frictional grip of, for example, the car seat as it prevents you following a straight-line path, tangential to the car's path.) Eventually, the cord will be fully unwound and impart no further acceleration to the bucket. At this point, bucket and water will have the same angular velocity, and the water surface maintains a constant concavity. If the bucket's motion is halted, the concavity will diminish as the water returns to rest. Hence, the period of *greatest* relative motion between bucket and water is accompanied by the *least* change in the water surface (i.e. at the very beginning of the experiment), and the period of *least* relative motion 'twixt water and bucket is accompanied with the *greatest* concavity in the water (i.e. when water and bucket rotate with the same velocity). These changes don't seemingly depend on relative motion between water and bucket, or between bucket and observer. (If you run round a stationary bucket of water, the water should exhibit no recessionary effects.) Thus, the relationalist has to explain: (1) why maximum recession of water occurs when there's zero relative velocity (i.e. when bucket and water are at rest relative to each other), and (2) why zero recessionary effect (i.e. the water surface is flat) occurs at greatest relative velocity between bucket and water (i.e. when the bucket is first released). Newton concluded that relationalism can't explain the observed facts and hence that recessionary forces imply that the water undergoes *absolute* rotation (i.e. relative, not to other physical bodies, but to space itself).[64]

§112 Berkeley adopts the formulation for absolute motion given by Newton, namely 'change of absolute place'. Berkeley says motion must be defined relative to some object. All statements like 'x moves' can be glossed 'x moves relative to a, b or c'. To say of a body that it moves, it must be possible to stipulate another body, relative to which the position or distance of the first body undergoes a change. This stipulation need not be explicit but nonetheless if a body moves, it must move relative to some other body. (So motion is relational and, as we heard at §89, relations are mind-dependent. Here the attack on absolute space joins up with the attack on material substance and absolute existence.)

§113 Berkeley rejects absolute motion but does distinguish real from apparent motions. Consider someone walking down a cobbled street. Usually, we would describe this as the walker's feet moving over the cobbles and not as the cobbles moving beneath the walker's feet. Why? Because the person's feet exert the force (not the cobbles). Berkeley distinguishes real from apparent motion thus: the *really* moving body is the one where force is applied. Although the conceivability of motion requires at least two bodies, Berkeley allows 'it may be that one only is moved'. The relation of motion between two bodies can be asymmetrical: 'As a man may think of somewhat which doth not think, so a body may be moved to or from another body, which is not therefore itself in motion.'

§114 Berkeley applies a 'conceivability' test to motion: we can only conceive of relative motion and we cannot form any idea of absolute motion, that is, motion without reference to any perceptible thing. In the light of his account of motion, Berkeley therefore rejects Newton's bucket argument because (perhaps surprisingly) he thinks the water is not truly moving: 'For the water in the vessel, at that time wherein it is said to have the greatest relative circular motion, hath, I think, no motion at all: as is plain from the foregoing section.' (NB Recall that Berkeley defines the truly moving body as the site of the impressed force.)

It has been claimed that Berkeley's views on space and scientific method resemble those which influenced Albert Einstein (1879–1955), via Ernst Mach (1838–1916), in producing relativity theory.[65] However, while Berkeley and Mach offer relationalist views of space, their philosophical responses to Newton's bucket experiment were rather different. Mach suggested that the relationalist might explain the bucket's inertial effects by appeal to the gravitational influence of distant stars:

> Newton's experiment with the rotating vessel of water simply informs us, that the relative rotation of the water with respect to the sides of the vessel produces *no* noticeable centrifugal forces, but that such forces *are* produced by its relative rotation with respect to the mass of the earth and the other celestial bodies.[66]

Where Mach outlined an alternative relationalist explanation for recessionary effects, Berkeley (in *PHK*) simply denies that the bucket actually moves.

§115 Berkeley now offers two conditions for calling 'a body *moved*': 'first, that it change its distance or situation with regard to some other body; and secondly, that the force or action occasioning that change be applied to it'. He reiterates that in the absence of either of prerequisites being fulfilled, a body cannot be meaningfully said to have moved. We can thus be mistaken in thinking a body is moving when in fact it isn't. (Like Newton's bucket.)

§116 Berkeley again attacks the notion of single ideas as determinate bearers of meaning: 'Though indeed we are apt to think every noun substantive stands for a distinct idea, that may be separated from all others; which hath occasioned infinite mistakes.' For example, if we examine any idea we can form of 'pure space', we find that all we can mean is 'For the limbs of my body to be moved on all sides without the least resistance: but if that too were annihilated, then there could be no motion and consequently no space.' However, besides the mistake of thinking that there must be a distinct existent idea or entity for every significant word, Berkeley points out there is also the opposite cardinal error – that is, using the same word to denote several different things but assuming that use of the same word must imply sameness of nature. (For example, using the word 'extension' to cover the radically different, in Berkeley's terms, kinds of extension that are presented to sight and to touch.)

§117 So, Berkeley concludes (a little prematurely perhaps) that he has seen off both absolute time and space. He rounds off his attack on Newtonian space by considering advantages to religion in dispensing with it. Berkeley maintains that abandoning absolute space frees us from a 'dangerous dilemma', thus: if we accept that absolute space is, for example, eternal and immutable, then we accept either that absolute space is God or something other than God is eternal and immutable. Both these alternatives have been upheld. Berkeley's *PC* 298 and 825 accuse Hobbes, Locke, Henry More and Spinoza, among others, of deifying space. The other alternative, that is, allowing a non-Divine being to be eternal and immutable, is that of Newton and his followers. This too Berkeley found unacceptable, since it allowed another substantial being that was coeval with God. Newton also incurred Berkeley's theological ire by referring to space as God's 'sensorium' or theatre of sensory impressions. Berkeley was not pleased at the seeming implication that God's infinite awareness needed anything like perception or a sense-organ. Finally, since extension is passive and God is all activity, locating space in God means placing extension (a purely inert quality), in a being who was the essence of power. Cf. 'It seems dangerous to suppose extension wch is manifestly inert in God' (*PC* 298).

Questions
1. Should final causes be banished from science and can science refrain entirely from metaphysical explanation?
2. Why should his idealism lead Berkeley to uphold relationalism about space?

3. Are Berkeley's counter-arguments to Newton's bucket experiment successful? Does Berkeley offer a genuine alternative explanation for recessionary effects, simply dismiss them out of hand or take another line of argument altogether?
4. Berkeley poses the Newtonian theist a dilemma: either absolute space possesses Divine attributes or there is another uncreated thing besides God. How might Berkeley's opponents escape this dilemma?

Mathematics (§§118–34)

Summary

Immaterialism's chief boon to mathematics is removing infinite divisibility. Berkeley argues that once infinite divisibility is gone, so too go the paradoxes of length and motion beloved of some philosophers. Besides contemporary debates over fluxions, Berkeley probably had in mind the paradoxes designed to prove the impossibility of motion, associated with Zeno of Elea (c. 475 BCE). In several of these arguments, infinity and infinite divisibility play key roles. (For example, Zeno's 'Achilles and the Tortoise' argument claims that the fastest runner in the world, that is, Achilles, cannot catch the slowest runner (i.e. the Tortoise) because to do so would involve carrying out an infinite number of sub-tasks in a finite time.[67]) To support this aim, Berkeley argues that 'every particular finite extension' is, and can only be, an idea present to the mind of a percipient and that whatever is perceived by the mind is perfectly transparent to it. Thus, the parts that we can conceive a line as possessing must be the only parts that it can possess. Infinite divisibility is neither conceivable nor necessary.

Section by section

§118 Turning now to advantages for mathematics, Berkeley begins by pointing out that, while mathematics rightly enjoys an unparalleled reputation for the clarity and certainty of its demonstrations, it needn't be immune thereby from lurking conceptual errors. In particular, while Berkeley does not dispute the truth of received mathematical axioms, he suspects that the reasonings of mathematicians have become infected with the doctrine of abstract general ideas.

§119 It has been claimed that arithmetic has for its primary subject abstract ideas of numbers. However, this is not so and the prevalence of this belief has led mathematicians astray into high-flown but obscure speculations. Some of the more supposedly elevated flights of mathematical thought, and in particular, attempts to resolve all of Nature into mathematical relationships, have taken mathematics far astray from matters of practical significance. However, mathematical enquiry ought to be subservient to practice and leads quickly to inanities if indulged in as pure speculation.[68]

§120 Unity as an abstract idea was sufficiently disposed of in §13 and the Introduction. However, a further conclusion follows: if number is defined as 'a collection of units' and an abstract idea of unity is impossible, then no number can consist of a combination of (abstract) ideas of unity. Thus, if numbers are taken apart from particulars (such as the things being numbered, the numerals we use to denote those numbers, the practical uses to which we put measurement and calculation, etc.), then arithmetic would literally have nothing for a subject. Hence the practical applications (and significations) of mathematics have to be primary.

§121 By way of explicating what the correct construal of numbers should be, Berkeley offers a potted history of the development of numerals. Originally perhaps, the utility of having an abbreviated form for denoting units led early people to employ a single stroke or point to signify a unit, and thence to combine as many strokes (or points) together as they wished to denote numbers of units (I, II, III, etc.). However, more economical ways were found of representing numbers, whereby a single character might stand in for many individual strokes. Finally, Arabic or Indian mathematicians made the leap to giving significance to the placing of numerals, so that the same numeral might have different significance accordingly as it was placed in different points of a sequence of numerals. This rule-governed recombination of signs to allow the same basic elements to express many different meanings is something that mathematics probably derived from language. (This power of significant recombination according to rules is something that Berkeley also maintains can be observed in the natural world, considered as a system of ideas installed by God as a language for 'talking' to his Creation. Cf. Berkeley's replies to the 'Why microstructure?' objection at §§60–2.)

§122 Thus, arithmetic considers signs for things, not the things being numbered themselves. However, as noted before (§19 and the Introduction), it's a mistake to assume that words which don't signify any particular ideas in the mind of their users must therefore signify abstract general ideas. Thus, Berkeley is cautioning here against assuming that general truths must therefore have abstract general ideas as the bearers of the meanings of those truths. Berkeley is also voicing a nominalist distrust of taking numbers to be abstract objects existing in their own right. This mistaken reification of numbers is every bit as erroneous and wont to generate sterile disputes as would be a similar tendency to take words in abstraction from things.

§123 From number, it's a natural step to consider extension. Berkeley states that extension 'considered as *relative*' is the subject of geometry. (The qualification 'considered as relative' is an addition to the 1734 edition of *PHK*.) Berkeley opposes any suggestion that any finite extension can be capable of division into infinitely many parts, and holds that the removal of this concept of infinite divisibility will remove paradoxes of length and motion. The assumption that all finite extensions can be divided infinitely is everywhere assumed and nowhere doubted but yet is but nowhere argued for either.

§124 Berkeley proceeds to argue that 'Every particular finite extension' is, and can only be, an idea present to the mind of a percipient. Berkeley reiterates that what is perceived by the mind is perfectly transparent to it (another echo here of the rejection of an imperceptible substratum, serving as an underpinning to what we perceive). Thus, the parts that we can conceive a line as possessing must be the only parts that it can possess.

§125 The doctrine of infinite divisibility is another unintended and pernicious consequence of the doctrine of abstract (general) ideas. Infinite divisibility can only be entertained (if at all) of ideas in the abstract. The notion that a line of an inch in length could nonetheless contain infinitely many parts is only sustainable if you already accept that extension can exist outside the mind, because clearly no perceivable object contains infinitely many parts. Geometricians are just as susceptible to abstractionist errors as everybody else, and it is to such errors that we owe the doctrine of infinite divisibility. (Admittedly, Berkeley did later relax his strictures on the conceivability of infinite parthood to the extent that he did account it at least a useful hypothesis for explications in geometry. Cf. *DM* 61: 'A curve can be considered as consisting of an infinite number of straight lines, though in fact it does not consist of them. That hypothesis is useful in geometry'.)

§126 Returning to a remark at Introduction §15, Berkeley glosses his statement that geometrical knowledge is 'conversant about universal ideas'. This doctrine needs to be expanded upon: the universal ideas in question are not abstract general ideas but rather ideas that become general by dint of being allowed to stand in for many other ideas of a similar kind. The geometer who uses a line of a certain length in constructing a proof may abstract from that particular line's particular length, but this abstraction simply involves paying no attention to the particular length when constructing the details of the proof. The geometer's ideas throughout will be determinate and will therefore have determinate particular magnitudes, but the proof need not pay attention to the precise magnitude at hand. (In Berkeley's own words, the geometer regards the particular length of the line as 'a thing indifferent to the demonstration'.) Thus, a geometer may speak of a 1-inch line as containing 10,000 parts, not because the geometer's idea of this line literally possesses 10,000 separate discriminable parts, but because the geometer uses the 1-inch line to do duty for a line with 10,000 component parts. So the line, although necessarily particular in itself, becomes 'universal only in its signification'. The (sadly common) error to watch for here is transferring those properties of the thing signified (in this case a line with 10,000 parts) to the thing which is doing the signifying (in this case the particular line of 1 inch in length), and therefore concluding that the properties imagined to reside in the thing signified must reside (intrinsically) in the signifier. (Perhaps another indication that Berkley was alert to the dangers of conflating sign and signified and, in particular, to the dangers of attributing the properties of the representation to that which is represented. Cf. Pitcher's objection to the 'Master Argument' of §§22–3.)

§127 Berkeley further diagnoses the mistaken belief in infinite divisibility thus: for any line that contains a determinate number of parts, a line can always be imagined which contains more parts. For any determinate number of parts you assign, no matter how high, you can always go higher still. Aristotle distinguished between the potentially infinite and the actually infinite. The former is an infinity which is formed over time, a process or object which can always have more added to it, while the latter is an infinity which is completed at a time, an actually finished infinite thing. Thus, Berkeley seems to allow that lines are only *potentially* infinite in the Aristotelian sense, that is, capable of being added to and added to indefinitely. However, like Aristotle, Berkeley rejects the idea that the physical world can contain anything which is *actually* infinite, that is, any thing that contains a completed infinity of parts or attributes.[69] Alas, in practice people often elide the distinction between infinities in sign and signified, concluding (wrongly) that the actual infinity attributed to the one must be found in the latter. A line does not become any greater in itself through being used to signify a line containing 10 parts or containing 10,000 parts.[70]

§128 So, when we would make a universal theorem, we are obliged to treat some particular line as though it contained parts that in fact it does not, or even cannot, contain. If we attended more closely to the ideas we form when asked to entertain the hypothesis that an inch can be divided into 1,000 parts, we might well find that we cannot actually entertain this idea about an inch. Instead, we may find that the idea we form is actually that of a line of far greater extent than an inch in length, and which an inch merely represents. Berkeley then claims, and it isn't entirely clear how this claim follows from what he's just said, that correctly understood, the claim that a line is infinitely divisible must mean that it contains infinitely many parts. In turn, the claim that a given line contains infinitely many parts must imply that the line is infinitely great. So, there can be no infinite divisibility of any length of less than infinite extent.

§129 Infinite divisibility has given rise to undesirable consequences, absurdities and contradictions. Berkeley sadly suspects that mathematicians are unwilling to let unfortunate consequences be admitted as arguments against mathematical doctrines. (As he puts it: 'But by I know not what logic, it is held that proofs *a posteriori* are not to be admitted against propositions relating to infinity.') As we've heard before, Berkeley lays great stress on *a posteriori* ('consequentialist') objections to materialism, that is, objections that seek to discredit materialism by laying unappealing consequences at materialism's door.

§130 Speculations in mathematics have lately been taken to what Berkeley regards as a dangerous and ridiculous level of abstraction, including the postulation of iterated infinitesimals. Thus, Berkeley remarks (rather scornfully) that some believe that not only may finite lengths be divided into infinitely many parts but that each of these (infinitely many) parts may itself be divided into infinitely many parts, and those parts in their turn may be divided, *ad infinitum*.[71] Others hold that anything below the first-order infinitesimals (i.e. the infinitely many parts of an initial finite length) are literally of zero extension.[72] Berkeley expresses some sympathy for this latter view, professing himself unable to understand how any non-zero extension can be multiplied infinitely many times and yet yield an extension of no greater than a fixed finite amount. However, he also remarks that it seems equally strange to accept the first-order infinitesimals but reject any higher-order infinitesimals, as though any non-zero quantity can yield an answer of zero through being multiplied by itself.[73]

§131 In the light of the above difficulties, the only correct solution is to foreswear the use of infinitesimals altogether. No part of geometrical practice will be adversely affected by this restriction.

§132 One might retort that the use of infinitesimals has been of great utility and that 'several theorems undoubtedly true' have been proved using them, which would seem difficult if the very notion of infinitesimal was contradictory. Berkeley replies that thorough examination will reveal that infinitesimals are not indispensable and that we need neither use nor even conceive of 'infinitesimal parts of finite lines'. (This remark of Berkeley's is left more as a promissory note than a developed argument in *PHK*, as he doesn't then go to demonstrate how those theorems that in fact were derived using infinitesimals could equally have been derived without their use.) Berkeley goes further however and states that not only are infinitesimals neither necessary nor useful in mathematical proof, in practice we will find that we need go no further down the road of resolving lengths into parts than the '*minimum sensible*'. This last is the Latin name for the smallest unit that we can perceive for any given sense, so, for example, the '*minimum visible*' would be the smallest-perceivable unit for sight. Berkeley talks more of *minima sensibilia* in the *NTV*, and even states at *NTV* 44 that the full moon is 30 visual *minima* in diameter. Whether or not Berkeley held that the visual field is literally composed of many visual points, each one *minimum visible* in diameter, is still debated. It has been argued that Berkeley's *minima* are merely the limit to which the size of visible objects can descend, or they are 'ways of seeing' and 'not to be thought of as units that compose or make up a sensory world'.[74]

§133 As noted above, the doctrine of matter has led to important errors. In particular, '*the absolute existence of corporeal objects*' has been a boon to irreligious belief.

§134 It does follow that if we reject the existence of matter, several thorny philosophical issues are also dismissed with it and some of these issues are held in high esteem as both difficult and serious. However, far from being a disadvantage of immaterialism, it seems to favour that doctrine if intellectual labour is reduced thereby.

Questions
1. Is Berkeley correct in claiming that all mathematical theory should be subservient to practical ends?
2. How widespread is the fallacy of thinking that the properties of the sign must also inhere in the signified? Does Berkeley himself ever succumb to this fallacy?
3. Does Berkeley's rejection of infinite divisibility really deliver mathematics and motion from paradoxes like those of the Eleatic Zeno?
4. If physical objects are only composed of sensible ideas and ideas in turn can only have the properties we perceive them as having, must Berkeley then accept that physical objects are literally composed of *minima sensibilia*?

Other minds (§§135–47)

Summary
If, as Berkeley admits, ideas can only resemble other ideas, we seemingly can't form any idea of spirit or active agency (cf. *PHK* 27). However, we can form a 'notion' of the mind. A notion is not like an idea, in that it does not offer any positively content-carrying picture of the thing denoted. Berkeley talks of our having *notions* of the operations of the mind or of the nature of God as opposed to *ideas* of those operations or of this nature.

If we can form no idea of spirit, any more than we can form an idea of matter, aren't spirit and matter then in exactly the same boat when it comes to concept formation – two substances neither of which we can properly imagine or conceptualize? However, Berkeley replies, the two cases are not parallel. We cannot form even a vague notion of an object where that object must embody a contradiction. Thus, while we can definitely form no ideas either of matter or of spirit, only the former can be rejected as a possible existent, because while any conception of spirit must fall short of its full active actuality, any conception we might form of matter is incoherent – a mere empty notion (cf. *PHK* 17). In later works, Berkeley considered the charge that, on his own principles, he should reject *both* material and mental substance, since he can form ideas of neither. Berkeley replies that while he can't form ideas of mind or matter, and can form only a notion of spirit, this notion is at least coherent, whereas he can form only a 'contradictory notion' of matter (*D* 232–3).

Granted we are not given ideas of other minds, we can still infer the existence of such minds through observing changes in the ideas we perceive. We can (and must) derive the notion of mind or spirit from direct attention to our selves, and then generalize this notion to other minds. The agency of God is omnipresent and provides the stable causal background that permits our grasp of other minds. Thus, any belief in other (finite) minds is (properly understood) dependent upon belief in God. Any grasp we have of the existence of other minds is rooted in the regularity of Nature and thus depends on God's sustaining goodness. (Here Berkeley argues for a personal, theistic God and not an impersonal First Cause.) Thus, belief in other minds is related to belief in God, but the latter belief is the more secure, since evidence of God's purposes is all-pervasive (see *PHK* 147). (In an aside at *PHK* 141, Berkeley discusses the immortality of the soul.)

Section by section

§135 Berkeley next considers our knowledge of spirits, which is generally thought to be deficient and imperfect. However, it is no defect in our understanding that we cannot form any idea of spirit. As such an idea is impossible, our failure to form such an idea cannot be held against us. (The Likeness Principle precludes inert ideas representing active spirits.)

§136 However, perhaps another kind of sense (hitherto unknown) could yield ideas of spirit, just as we now have (visual) ideas of triangles through using our sight. As in §77 (when discussing a hypothetical extra sense that yielded ideas of material substance), Berkeley points out that all a new sense could do would be to furnish us with new ideas of an unfamiliar kind; it could not give us ideas of anything that by its very nature could not resemble an idea. Spirit is active, where no passive idea can resemble (or represent) anything active, and therefore our faculties can no more be faulted for failing to give us ideas of spirit than they could be for failing to give us ideas of 'a round square'.

§137 The doctrine that spirits could be apprehended via ideas has had unfortunate philosophical and religious consequences. Berkeley speculates that many may have been led to scepticism about the existence of the soul through trying and failing to find any idea of it. Indeed, Berkeley seems quite mystified at why such attempts have ever been made, since he takes it as a conceptual (or necessary) truth that an idea (whose *esse* is *percipi*) cannot resemble a spirit (whose *esse* is *percipere*). Still, Berkeley imagines a further challenge: even if idea cannot resemble (and hence represent) spirits in respect of spirits' activity, maybe idea can resemble spirits in *some* respect. We don't specify that a sign must resemble the signified in absolutely *all* respects.

§138 Berkeley replies that there are certain resemblances which representation must capture if it is to be representation at all. (One might claim that any 'representation' of a square that failed to refer to properties like four-sidedness or being a plane figure failed as a representation.) If we omit willing, thinking and perceiving from any (putative) representation of spirit, we are left with no representation of spirit at all. So, if we grant that no idea can resemble these activities, no idea can represent a spirit.

§139 The next objection is this: even if we grant that ideas cannot represent spirits, this reply offers only a Pyrrhic victory for idealism because 'spirit' is robbed of all meaning. Berkeley replies to this that the word 'spirit' has a sufficiently clear sense to it, being the same as the thing he denominates 'I', even though no idea is associated with the name.

If we were to broaden the meaning of 'idea' to encompass all those things that names can immediately signify then in that (rather diluted) sense of 'idea', Berkeley would grant that we can have an 'idea' of spirit. Interestingly, Berkeley takes the meaningfulness of 'spirit' as a given and effectively says: the case of spirit is a clear exception to the principle that every meaningful name must have an idea annexed to it. (He might also have reiterated that not all significant words must have ideas annexed to them, or that the only function of language is relaying ideas.) However, Berkeley insists this dispute over ideas versus notions of spirit is not merely verbal. We must distinguish spirits from ideas 'to prevent equivocation and confounding natures perfectly disagreeing and unlike'.

§140 Berkeley considers further broadening 'idea' to include any subject of meaningful discourse. Again, in such a *broad* sense, we have an 'idea' of spirit, because we can use the term in well-formed utterances. However, Berkeley believes that strictly we have a *notion* of spirit, and not an idea. A notion is the product of reflection rather than imagination or perception. (Cf. Philonous: 'I say lastly that I have a notion of spirit, though I have not, strictly speaking, an idea of it. I do not perceive it as an idea or by means of an idea, but know it by reflection', *D* 233.) Likewise, Berkeley talks of our having *notions* (as opposed to ideas) of the mind's operations or of God's nature. Just as we can know that other minds exist through forming a notion of their perceptions modelled on our own ideas, so we can know what goes on in other minds by a similar process of analogy. Our notion of our own spirit bears the same similarity to our notions of other spirits that our perceptual ideas bear to the perceptual ideas of other minds. This series of resemblances seem more metaphorical than convincing however and leaves a lot of work to be done by the (sketchily defined) 'notions'.

Although a popular, seemingly commonsensical and enduring strategy for solving the problem of how we can know that other minds exist and have experiences like ours, this kind of argument by analogy has subsequently been heavily criticized and is more or less universally regarded as hopelessly flawed. All such arguments face the problem that the resulting conclusion is at best very weakly supported by its premises, if we are really inferring to the nature and existence of all other minds purely from observing our own case and then generalizing it. We can access the contents of only one mind directly (i.e. our own) and must then use this single-case access as a basis from which to generalize to all the other minds we think there are, and have been, in existence. In the wake of Wittgenstein's 'Private Language Argument', philosophers have concluded that the argument from analogy misrepresents how we justify our knowledge of other minds.[75] If I were to make the claim that solipsism is true, that is, that I am the only mind that there is, the possibility of this utterance only makes sense if there is a public language for me to express it in. In turn the possibility of a public language is itself parasitic upon the existence of a public, rule-governed context for that language. So then, rather than being a *hypothesis* that we support by analogical reasoning and empirical evidence, the existence of other minds (plus a rule-governed social background for language) seems better construed as an inescapable assumption if we are to possess meaningful utterances. In other words, arguments from analogy misunderstand scepticism about other minds. Such scepticism is not an empirical hypothesis that we can gather evidence for or against but rather a metaphysical hypothesis of such sceptical breadth that it becomes self-defeating. To have the resources to be able to express 'other minds' scepticism or solipsism, you need to assume that there are public and interpretable rules that govern language. Hence solipsism would be a self-defeating hypothesis, even if all other minds were to drop out of existence.

Even as arguments from analogy go, Berkeley's argument may be particularly vulnerable, due to the removed and weakened analogy Berkeley permits between one's own mind and that of another. Only in a rather weak sense does Berkeley grant that our spirit may 'resemble' other spirits, in that both can be made subjects of hypothetical resemblance. The above isn't satisfactory though, not least because Berkeley asks us to accept a resemblance between two things that we cannot compare directly (i.e. our own mind and other minds) on the strength of its similarity to another resemblance between a different pair of things that we can't compare (i.e. the ideas we perceive and the ideas that other minds perceive).

§141 Next, the immortality of the soul. Berkeley's grounds for thinking the soul immortal are rather Cartesian, for example, 'the soul is indivisible, incorporeal, unextended, and it is consequently incorruptible'. To claim the soul is immortal is not to claim that the soul is *absolutely* indestructible, that is, incapable of destruction even by the direct intervention of God. Rather, it is to claim that soul cannot suffer death or disintegration as the result of any natural process. (The Cartesian soul is an indivisible mental substance which can survive independently of any body. According to Descartes, souls are immune from ageing or decay, cannot dissolve or split into parts and can be destroyed only 'by God's denying his concurrence to them'.[76] Barring direct Divine volitions to the contrary, Cartesian souls should survive death forever.) However, *contra* Descartes and Berkeley alike, indivisibility does not guarantee immortality and the inference from indivisibility to immortality is not obviously valid: 'It does not follow from a soul's being indivisible that it cannot lose its capacity for experience and action – and so cease to be a soul.'[77] Granted, Berkeley argues that souls must always think, but his argument seems to assume that any other existence for the mind would have absurd consequences, like discontinuous existence and/or continual re-creation. (In other words, here again Berkeley argues *a posteriori*, from consequences.)

In any event, Berkeley claims to find continuous creation acceptable enough (*vide* §46) so why not accept continuous re-creation? Perhaps Berkeley felt that continuous re-creation threatens the identity of the person. Radical conclusions about personal identity were sometimes derived from the continuous creation doctrine in the eighteenth century. Jonathan Edwards

(1703–58)[78] argued that no object can endure through time by any power of its own and hence every object must be re-created anew at every instant. Hence, every instant marks a new creation of the universe which represents as profound a break from its previous state as the original Creation was. It follows that every object consists of radically discrete temporal parts, and has no parts in common with that object at any other time. Edwards invoked this doctrine to defend God's visiting punishment for original sin on Adam's descendants, because 'it is as reasonable and just to impute Adam's original sin to me now as it is to impute any sin which I may seem to remember having committed myself'.[79]

Berkeley thinks a further advantage of immaterialism is that it reduces the risk of scepticism about the soul's immortality. Berkeley doesn't mention Hobbes by name here but his remarks about those 'who hold the soul of man to be only a sort of thin vital flame, or system of animal spirits' seem clearly aimed at Hobbesian materialists. Berkeley maintains that reducing the soul to any material form makes scepticism about survival of death almost inevitable, 'since nothing is more easily dissipated than such a being'. If however the soul is a mental substance then there is no reason why the body's natural decay should affect the (active and uncompounded) soul in the slightest.

§142 Berkeley returns to the impossibility of forming an idea of the soul, specifically dismissing the possibility that any augmentation of, or addition to our senses, could yield such an idea. He likens the impossibility of forming a (passive) idea of the (active) spirit to that of hoping to '*see a sound*'. Again, he appeals to our having a notion of the soul, where to have a notion of entity X is to understand what is meant by the name 'X'. He extends the use of notions to include our knowledge of relations. This is because, in line with his generally nominalist (and particularist) suspicion of universals and intrinsically general abstract ideas, Berkeley maintains that all relations are mind-dependent. Thus, a relation is created only by the act of a mind and such acts cannot be represented by passive ideas. (Cf. Berkeley's account of the mind-dependence of number, at §12.)

§143 Once again, the doctrine of abstract ideas has misled philosophers, this time with regard to the spirit. Another abstractionist error is that of thinking that we can form abstract ideas of the acts or powers of the mind, even of the mind itself, which are independent of any ideas of the objects and effects (i.e. ideas) of consciousness.

§144 But perhaps the greatest error with regard to the soul is illegitimately transferring to our discussions of the soul terms which are derived from our ideas of sensible things. For example, talk of the will as 'the *motion* of the soul' is to misapply an idea which only has significance when applied to a sensible thing. Any notion that the soul is, or can be, impelled or forced by a mere sensible quality like motion is to import into discussions of the mind a non-transferable mechanical model of explanation and thus to invite the downgrading of the mind to a sort of deterministic machine. Such mechanical theories of the soul have dangerous moral consequences. Thus Berkeley is clearly what philosophers would now call a libertarian incompatibilist about free will, that is, one who believes that human freedom and determinism are irreconcilable doctrines and who embraces the reality of freedom while rejecting that of determinism. The physical world depends for its existence on the operations of Mind and cannot therefore determine those operations. A determinist incompatibilist (or 'hard determinist') believes that human freedom and determinism are irreconcilable doctrines and accepts determinism but denies human freedom. Hume, by contrast, was a compatibilist about free will and maintained that human freedom actually presupposes the thesis of determinism. Hume also raised sceptical worries about freedom as it relates to the substance of the mind – in Hume's view, events in a purely mental substance might be every bit as subject to casual determinism as material events. (See *Treatise* 2/3/1.)

§145 Our knowledge of other minds, and even of their very existence, is necessarily confined to their operations or to the ideas that they excite in us. Thus, our knowledge of other minds is mediate (or inferential), unlike our immediate knowledge of our own ideas. However, we are not thereby reduced to scepticism about the existence and properties of other minds. For all that we cannot literally perceive the workings of any mind, whether our own or anyone else's, we can see still perceive the characteristic effects of mind. These effects include regular sequences and combinations of sensible ideas. I observe combinations of ideas like those I can generate myself and I therefore infer that such like effects have like causes. Thus, knowledge of other minds is different from knowledge of our own minds; the latter is immediate, whereas the former requires the intervention of ideas, which we then attribute to other spirits as the signs or accompaniments of such spirits.

§146 Some of the combinations of sensible ideas we observe can be attributed to the action of minds like our own. However, the vast majority of such combinations cannot be attributed to human agency but invite (or demand) the postulation of a spirit of much greater power, wisdom and resource than any human being. However powerful the evidence for the existence of other (finite) spirits, this evidence pales beside that for the existence of a transcendental spirit of vastly more than human power and wisdom. The steadfastness with which the visual ideas of, for example, the rising Sun are correlated with tactile ideas of heat may *resemble* the sorts of arrangement of ideas we can achieve in artificial language, but the order of Nature exceeds anything we could achieve to such a degree that it indicates the existence and continuing activity of a spirit of infinite goodness, power and wisdom.

For this argument to succeed, Berkeley needs to appeal to our own experience as providing a sustainable model of agency. We need to know when and how we can act as causes in order to know that we are not the causes of all our own perceptual ideas. (Thus, there is also a link between Berkeley's account of agency and any resources he might have for defeating solipsism.) Here again is a point of disagreement with Malebranche. Where Malebranche believed God was the only true cause, Berkeley believed that finite spirits too could possess genuine causal powers. Berkeley explicitly rejected Malebranche's doctrine of the causal inefficacy of the will from an early stage of his career (e.g. 'We move our Legs our selves. 'tis we that will their movement. Herein I differ from Malbranch', *PC* 548). Berkeley not only held that causation by finite spirits was intelligible; he thought our experience of agency afforded the only model of causation we could understand.

§147 Any grasp we have of the existence of other minds is ultimately rooted in the regularity of Nature and thus depends on the existence of God. Thus, belief in other minds is closely related to belief in God, but the latter belief is on the more secure footing, since evidence of God's purposes is all-pervasive:

> Hence it is evident that God is known as certainly and immediately as any other mind or spirit whatsoever, distinct from ourselves. We may even assert, that the existence of God is far more evidently perceived than the existence of men. . . . For it is evident that in affecting other persons, the will of man hath no other object, than barely the motion of the limbs of his body.

Our evidence for God's existence is if anything stronger than (because our evidence is effectively parasitic upon) that for the existence of other human minds.

However, a new problem arises: if God is the supreme agent and the natural world, the theatre of our actions, depends on his causal maintenance, is not God then the author of all moral evil and indeed all human actions whatsoever? Are immaterialists not then forced into hard deterministic or fatalistic rejection of our moral responsibility? Berkeley's reply is essentially that the 'culpable God' and 'fatalism' objections misstate the relationship between human and Divine action. Whatever resources a person may have for affecting the generation of ideas in other minds is confined to what that person can control via volitions. In turn, those portions of the world which are under a person's direct control are basically confined to the movements of that person's limbs. However, the stable causal background, the system of regular and predictable natural laws, which makes it possible for us to transmit our ideas and intentions to each other, is dependent upon the will (and continuing benevolence) of God. God provides the blackboard, if you like, on which human volitions can write their chalky messages.[80]

Questions
1. Do we really lack all idea of mind? If so, is a 'notion' of spirit enough?
2. Does Berkeley draw a sufficiently principled difference between the vague notion of spirit and the contradictory notion of mind?

3. Is Berkeley's way of arguing for the existence of other minds an argument from analogy? If so, how good an analogy is it?
4. Is the existence of God really on a better evidential footing than that of finite minds? Does belief in other minds presuppose belief in God?

The divine language of nature (§§148–56)

Summary

Our ideas of sense exhibit an order which invites comparison with the finest ordering we observe in human artefacts, but with vastly greater sophistication and on a vastly greater scale. Ideas can only reside in minds and so Berkeley thinks that the ordering of sensory ideas must have been performed by a gigantic agent intelligence. God's purposes are manifested to us in a regular world and God has so related the ideas of the different senses that ideas from one sense can serve as signals for what we can expect from another. In both natural and human languages, no sign has an intrinsic meaning and all links between signs are conventional. Just as finite human agents can create systems of artificial signs in languages, so God's infinite agency has created a vastly greater and more suggestive natural language. (Cf. *NTV* 147: 'The proper objects of vision constitute an universal language of the Author of Nature, whereby we are instructed how to regulate our actions in order to attain those things that are necessary to the preservation and well-being of our bodies, as also to avoid whatever may be hurtful and destructive of them.')[81] God created Nature as a system of ideas for finite minds to read and to understand, and science exists to express this order as economically and comprehensively as possible. *PHK* closes with a review of the religious and moral advantages to be gleaned from a correct (immaterialist) understanding of the world and our place therein.

Section by section

§148 Through the manifestation of God's purposes in the regularity of the world and the sensory appearances we experience, we have a direct presentation of God and God's purposes, which should make any temptation to atheism unintelligible: 'We do at all times and in all places perceive manifest tokens

of the divinity; everything we see, hear, feel or any wise perceive by sense, being a sign or effect of the Power of God.' In
effect, nature is a Divine Language, which reveals purposes to
us (albeit a language in which we are spoken to rather more
than we can speak.) However, Berkeley's view of God as mani-
festing through the regularity of Nature is neither pantheist or
Malebranchean:

> Not that I imagine we see God (as some will have it) by a
> direct and immediate view, or see corporeal things, not by
> themselves, but by seeing that which represents them in
> the essence of God, which doctrine is I must confess to me
> incomprehensible.

According to Malebranche, the idea of extension could not be
grasped directly by the unaided human mind. However, God
can so exert his powers that on particular occasions, the Divine
idea of extension can be made a possible object of human cognition: 'For all our clear ideas are in God in their intelligible
reality. It is only in him that we see them. Do not imagine that
what I say here is new. It is the opinion of St. Augustine.'[82]

§149 It is therefore obvious that God not only exists but
directs and governs the natural world, and is therefore intimately involved in the maintenance of the world.

§150 Doesn't Berkeley's doctrine deny the role of Nature in
producing natural things, and instead ascribe all causality to
'the immediate and sole operation of God'? No, there remains
room for intervention in the world by the causal efforts of finite
agents too. (Here is a crucial respect in which Berkeley differs
from Malebranche – the latter, as noted above, denying that
there could be any causal powers in any entity save God.)

§151 But surely the production of natural effects is a very long
and slow process? This gradualism seems *prima facie* incom-
patible with the direct instigation and governance of a Divine
agent. There are also many examples of imperfect and disas-
trous productions of nature, with much attendant suffering – all
of which suggest that Nature is (at the very least) not under
God's direct governance and control. In reply, Berkeley refers
back to *PHK* §62 and reiterates that the methods of Nature are
chosen by God in order that natural effects might follow from

their causes in a law-like and regular way. God chooses 'the most simple and general rules' by which to manage Nature; and does not interrupt the regularity of His own handiwork with irregular supernatural irruptions. Nature is like a vast mechanism, whose Maker has so ordered it that the mechanism can be left to run apparently by itself, without the need for obvious and repeated adjustment. Without the regular sequences of events that constitutes Nature, human life and action, even the exercise of human cognition, would be impossible. Thus, although the regular sequence of Nature will produce short-term and localized accidents or other suffering, the benefits conferred on us by this regularity far outweigh the occasional ill effects. This is essentially Berkeley's answer to the 'problem of evil', namely how to reconcile the existence of an all-good, all-wise and all-powerful God with the existence of seemingly needless suffering. Thus, God does not will evil directly; instead, God wills that there be regularity in Nature. Although God presumably knows that such regularity will (indirectly) cause suffering, the suffering is greatly outweighed by the possibility of shared purposes and communication that the regularity of Nature permits.

§152 Having offered a general justification for the apparent existence of imperfections in Nature, Berkeley goes on to argue that even apparent imperfections in nature might also have their uses, in affording variety. We should be careful in imputing any extravagance of effect, or ill adaptation of means to ends, to God. It is not safe to generalize from our own limited methods of production and thereby legislate for the methods God should follow. Economy of effort is a virtue and a sign of wisdom in (finite) human minds; however, God can choose any means He thinks fit to achieve His ends. The resources of omnipotence are not constrained to choose (what might seem to us) the most economical means of working. This point may be in some tension with Berkeley's earlier strictures against Malebranchean occasionalism and the general explanatory redundancy of matter. Thus, it's really the arguments designed to establish the incoherence of material substance and its epistemic inaccessibility that form the strongest cards in Berkeley's hand. After all, one can imagine a theist materialist retorting, if matter could exist, why shouldn't God choose to use material substance as an occasional cause if it seemed fit to God so to do? The argument for the explanatory redundancy of matter thus also needs to be bolstered with Berkeley's argument that God could never require an instrument to achieve his purposes. Omnipotence cannot require any instrument, because infinite power can accomplish all possible things directly.

The Divine Language model of Nature also furnishes Berkeley with another objection to the existence of imperceptible, Newtonian absolute space. If the ideas of sense are part of a gigantic language, then any set of appearances which cannot be conjoined can form no part of the natural language of signs and hence cannot be found in nature. The natural world is a system of correlated signs and nothing more. To be unimaginable is to fail a crucial test for existence. Thus, if the imagination can frame nothing which would answer to the conjunction of a certain group of signs, this suffices to deny the possibility of that conjunction of signs actually obtaining. Thus, the Divine Language model relates Berkeley's philosophy of science and attack on absolute space to his conceivability criterion of possibility and (indirectly) the Master Argument too.

However, not all Berkeley's commentators have found the Divine Language model of Nature consoling. For example, D. M. Armstrong thinks Berkeley's doctrine of signs threatens what he calls 'cosmic epoch' scepticism, that is, that the laws we observe in our section of the universe are not invariant across all spatio-temporal conditions. Our laws may be true only of an isolated segment of space-time, leaving us with no warrant to extrapolate from our observations to exceptionless laws for the universe at large. Given that only the express *fiat* of God orders the world, we have no reason to think that the contingent relations we observe between signs now will persist or are typical of the correlations that have obtained: 'If it seemed best to him, he could abrogate the so-called "laws of nature" tomorrow'.[83] Berkeley would surely reply to this that entertaining this possibility mistakes the nature of God's relationship to the world. In theory, God could suspend the laws of nature and institute new ones (rewriting the grammar of the language of Nature as it were), but such would belie the reasons for creating the system of Nature in the first place. God's purposes provide the explanation for the stability of nature and a guarantee that such stability will continue.

§153 Berkeley further bolsters his reply to the problem of evil by trying to reduce our propensity to dwell on suffering. Perhaps, he argues, our mulling over the problem of evil is a function of our overconcentration on particular privations or injuries. If we took a larger view of Nature, we might find that the apparent needlessness of injuries and disasters would disappear and we would become more easily reconciled to the apparent needless suffering in the world if we could better grasp the various ways in which objects and natural laws are interlinked by God to conduce to our overall benefit.

At the risk of stretching a point, perhaps any failure on the part of his readers to appreciate Berkeley's solution to the problem of evil is something else that Berkeley might diagnose as an unfortunate instance of overabstraction. We tend to concentrate on *particular* instances of suffering abstracted from the general, natural regularities that may (indirectly) create suffering but that are essential if human life is to be possible. Just as shape and extension are really inseparable, so too are the possibility of human discourse and the regularity of nature. God directly wills that Nature should be regular, while the regularity of Nature (indirectly and occasionally) leads to suffering.[84]

§154 Berkeley concludes that the foregoing review of arguments for, and advantages in, immaterialism leaves only two possible explanations for a decision to embrace atheism or Manicheanism. (The Manichean explains the mixture of goodness and suffering in the world by postulating two supernatural principles, one good and one evil. These principles are coeval and neither one proceeds from, nor can be reduced to, the other. Thus, Manicheans accept a theological dualism, not to be confused with mind/body substance dualism. Christianity on the other hand, is a theologically monistic faith: there is one all-powerful supernatural principle and that principle is supremely good, wise and powerful.) These explanations are 'want of attention and comprehensiveness of mind'. A little application and largeness of mind will reveal so many signs of the evident care and design with which Nature has been ordered, that unbelief should be impossible thereafter.

§155 Given how clear the evidence of God's existence and goodness is, it's more remarkable that people neglect taking steps to investigate the possible truth of Christianity, than that having failed to make any such investigation, they failed to be convinced of Christianity's truth.

§156 Berkeley closes Part I of *PHK* with a reminder to the reader of what he would like to have achieved in writing this work. Our aims should be primarily towards God and our duty and Berkeley would account his work a failure if it does not encourage his readers to accept a sense of the Divine presence. The end of successful philosophy should be to make a difference for the better in how we live and practice, not merely in how we think or debate.

Questions

1. Should we expect that God chooses to achieve His ends by what (at least to us) would seem the most economical means? If not, is there a tension between theism and Ockham's famous razor?
2. How useful is Berkeley's attempted solution to the problem of evil? Does it diminish God's omnipotence to hold that the best available way that Nature could be regulated produces suffering?
3. If Berkeley's aims are to restore his readers to practical action, what practical difference might contemplating the arguments of the *PHK* make?

CHAPTER 4

RECEPTION AND INFLUENCE

The initial reception of *PHK* was very disappointing for Berkeley. Judging from letters he wrote after early reactions to *PHK*, Berkeley particularly resented suggestions that he espoused immaterialism solely as a novelty. However, not all of Berkeley's early critics dismissed *PHK* through ignorance of philosophy, slavish adherence to Newtonianism or even knee-jerk hostility to immaterialism. One early reader of *PHK* was an idealist, a relationalist about space and a philosophical genius, but nonetheless wrote of Berkeley 'I suspect he belongs to that genus of men that wants to be known for paradoxes.'[1]

As Berkeley said, had he simply wished to achieve notoriety via paradoxes, he would have rushed into publication without troubling himself to anticipate objections:

Two imputations there are which (how unjust soever) I appre-hended would be charged on me by censorious men, and I find it has happened accordingly. The first, that I was not myself convinced of the truth of what I writ, but from a vain affectation of novelty designed imposing on the world :— whereas there is nothing I esteem more mean and miserable, I may add more wicked, than an intention to cheat men into a belief of lies and sophisms merely for the sake of a little reputation with fools. . . . I may add that the opinion of matter I have entertained some years ; if therefore a motive of vanity could have induced me to obtrude falsehoods on the world, I had long since done it when the conceit was warm in my imagination, and not have staid to examine and revise it both with my own judgement and that of my ingenious friends. The second imputation I was afraid of is, that men rash in their censures, and that never considered my book would be apt to confound me with the sceptics, who doubt of the existence of sensible things and are not positive to any one truth, . . . but whoever reads my book with due attention will plainly see that there is a direct opposition betwixt the principles contained in it and those of the sceptics, and that I question not the existence of anything that we perceive by our senses. (Rand, 1914, pp. 82–3)

While Berkeley's contemporaries often adopted (indeed celebrated) his account of vision, his essential philosophical arguments were often misdescribed, parodied or dismissed out of hand during his lifetime. However, as succeeding generations of philosophers arose, the image of Berkeley as trifling sceptic or mere purveyor of ingenious paradoxes gradually gave way to that of Berkeley the dedicated proponent of a novel and ingenious metaphysical system. This pattern of initial puzzlement, condescension or silence, gradually succeeding to critical discussion and acclaim, was paralleled in the career of Hume, whose *Treatise* 'fell dead-born from the press' on first publication in 1739 and 1740.[2] Hume concluded that his lack of success arose from the manner of his presentation rather than shortcomings in reasoning, and recast his *Treatise* into his two *Enquiries* (rather as Berkeley was to recast the doctrines of *PHK* of 1710 to make *D* in 1713).

Although heavily indebted to Berkeley in several respects, Thomas Reid (1710–96) concluded that Berkeley was effectively (although unwittingly) a sceptic and that the key misstep in his project was one that Berkeley had inherited from Cartesian and Lockean forerunners.[3] This key error Reid diagnosed as the doctrine that we are given direct contact via perception only with ideas. Granted this 'ideism', Reid thought the way was left clear for Locke's mitigated scepticism about matter, Berkeley's rejection of matter and Hume's rejection of (substantial) mind and matter alike. Thus, Berkeley undermined the representationalism of Locke by showing how it led to scepticism about material substance, and then Hume completed the sceptical descent of the empiricists by using (essentially) Berkeley's arguments to undermine belief in self, substance and God.

Berkeley did however find a sympathetic and able American correspondent in Samuel Johnson, who became a disciple of Berkeleyan immaterialism. Berkeley's influence can be felt in the subsequent history of American philosophy in general and particularly in the development of pragmatism. William James (1842–1910) claimed that pragmatism effectively aimed to do for the notion of truth what Berkeley did for the notion of physical existence: namely, stripping away inessential metaphysical baggage and applying standards of verification and evidence.[4] Charles Sanders Peirce (1839–1914) cited Berkeley as a major influence and was moved to offer a modified idealism, what Peirce's correspondent, Josiah Royce (1855–1916) called 'objective idealism'.[5]

Taking their cue largely from Reid and Immanuel Kant (1724–1804), many nineteenth-century historians of philosophy classified their seventeenth- and eighteenth-century predecessors as empiricists or rationalists. In such histories, Berkeley often figures as the middle term in the tripartite series of British empiricists that begins with Locke and culminates in Hume. In its favour, this traditional grouping of Berkeley with Locke and Hume does lay due weight on the strongly empiricist strand in Berkeley's thinking. However, this traditional grouping is also misleading if it leads to a neglect of the Cartesian and especially Malebranchean antecedents of many of Berkeley's doctrines.

Hume's debts to Berkeley are many. He was much impressed by Berkeley's attack on abstract ideas: 'I look upon this to be one of the greatest and most valuable discoveries that has been made of late years in the republic of letters' (*Treatise* 1/1/7).[6] Hume's *Treatise* theory of space rejected infinite divisibility (*Treatise* I/II/4) and Hume held that 'We have therefore no idea of space or extension, but when we regard it either as an object of our sight or feeling' (*Treatise* I/II/3). Likewise, his account of causation bears a strong resemblance to Berkeley's. Even Hume's 'bundle' theory of the self, although a view of a kind that Berkeley considered and rejected, has a strongly Berkeleyan inspiration. Many commentators (including Reid) held that Hume pushed Berkeleyan suspicion of material substance to its logical conclusion by being sceptical of the notion of substance in general and that of the self in particular. However, while Berkeley might have recognized in Hume a fellow empiricist of great analytical skill and pungency, he would have been appalled at the uses Hume made of his principles, and especially by Hume's general scepticism towards revealed and natural religion. Berkeley would scarcely have welcomed what happened to the Argument from Design at Hume's hands in his *Dialogues Concerning Natural Religion*. While there is far more to Hume than simply Berkeley without God, the godless strand of empiricist and phenomenalist thinking proved influential.

John Stuart Mill (1806–73), besides being a canonical figure in the development of utilitarianism and the philosophy of political liberalism, was in many ways a nineteenth-century phenomenalist heir to Berkeley. It was Mill, for example, who first proposed an analysis of material objects as 'permanent possibilities of sensation', an analysis of great importance in the development of phenomenalism.[7] Likewise, Berkeley's analogical way of arguing for the existence of other minds from our experiences of the connections between our own ideas and experiences was later taken up, and developed, by Mill. (Although Mill held that his argument was better than a merely analogical one, because it appealed to the explanatory value in postulating that similar outward behaviour was linked to, and generated by, similar inward states.)[8] Mill's phenomenalism rejected the theological doctrines Berkeley held dear and thoroughly expunged God from his philosophical system. J. L. Austin may owe Berkeley an indirect debt, via Mill, in that it seems to have been Austin's rejection of phenomenalism that drove him towards ordinary language philosophy.[9]

The history of logical positivism, at least in English-speaking philosophical circles, owes much to Berkeley's distinction between scientific and metaphysical explanation. A. J. Ayer (1910–89) cites Berkeley with approval in *Language, Truth and Logic* (London, 1936), claiming that the logical positivism espoused therein derives directly from empiricism as practised by Berkeley and Hume. However, it seems unlikely that Berkeley would have appreciated this acknowledgement, as Ayer rejected theistic metaphysics as meaningless and advanced a form of non-cognitivist expressivism about ethics. Berkeley's insistence on a strict demarcation between scientific description and metaphysical explanation does ally him with twentieth-century movements in philosophy of science like verificationism and logical positivism. However, his insistence that metaphysics is a higher calling than science would not have commended itself to verificationists or positivists, who generally held that metaphysics was at best dispensable and at worst meaningless.

The impact of Berkeley on the history of idealism in general has been as much one of reaction against as it has been one of agreement with, his central tenets. Kant took Berkeley as the paradigm of what he called 'subjective idealism', which confines our knowledge to objects as perceived by the subject, which Kant rejected in favour of his own *transcendental* idealism. Kant sought to bridge the empiricist and rationalist traditions, arguing that while our knowledge of particulars can only come through the senses, the unity of cognition and sense perception is only possible given certain categories of cognition that are given to us *a priori* (i.e. in the sense of prior to experience). Kant distinguished between the realm of appearances (or phenomenal world) and the realm of things-in-themselves (or noumenal world). The phenomenal world and its properties (like spatio-temporal order) are empirically real but transcendentally ideal.[10] We can form no positive knowledge of the noumenal realm, beyond that fact that such a realm distinct from the phenomenal world (probably) exists. What the relationship between noumenal and phenomenal realms might be is unclear – for example, such a relation cannot be causal, since causation is a spatio-temporal category. In turn, space and time are *a priori* particulars, or pure categories (and hence invariant features) of perception, but don't apply to the noumenal realm.[11] Kant held that Berkeley did not pay sufficient attention to the role that *a priori* (i.e. prior to experience) categories play in providing the structure that lets experience (and hence empirical knowledge) be possible.

British idealism became somewhat more rationalistic in the nineteenth century. The movement called 'British Idealism' began in the nineteenth century, with adherents including T. H. Green (1836–82), F. H. Bradley (1846–1924), Bernard Bosanquet (1848–1923) and J. M. E. McTaggart (1866–1925). This movement took its inspiration less from Berkeley and more from German Idealism in general and Hegel's Absolute Idealism in particular.[12] McTaggart was an immaterialist who held that the ultimate constituents of the universe are immortal selves, continuously perceiving themselves and each other. However, McTaggart's system was also (in sharp contrast to Berkeley's) atheistic.[13] Again in sharp contrast to Berkeley, McTaggart argued for the unreality of time, and hence that our perception of time was systematically misleading.[14] In its various Kantian and Hegelian forms, idealism seems to have become a doctrine which only rather tenuously resembles the common sense, direct realist idealism of Berkeley. If Kant could be allowed to baptize Berkeley's idealism retrospectively as 'subjective' or 'dogmatic', one can imagine Berkeley might equally dub Kantians and Hegelians adherents of 'sceptical' or 'occult' idealism.[15]

Modern empiricism about the philosophy of science has a rather ambiguous relationship with forebears like Berkeley. Nancy Cartwright, for example, finds inspiration in a form of pre-classical empiricism about causation, which she attributes to Joseph Glanvill (1636–80): 'In a sense I will be returning to an early form of British empiricism uncontaminated by the Cartesian doctrine of ideas, an empiricism where causal connections not only made sense but where they were in principle observable'.[16] Approvingly, Cartwright cites Joseph Glanvill on Adam's senses:

His sight could inform him whether the Loadstone doth attract by Atomic Effluviums; . . .. The Mysterious influence of the Moon, and its causality on the seas motion, was no question in his Philosophy, no more than a Clocks motion, is in ours, where our senses inform us of its cause.[17]

Thus, pre-classical empiricism (before the Cartesian ideist infection) saw nothing intrinsically problematic in observing causal relations. According to Glanvill, the pre-lapsarian eye could discern unmediated causal connections, and it is to this conception of 'causings' as directly perceptible that Cartwright wishes scientific empiricism to return. Gabriel Moked claims that Berkeley himself became a late convert to corpuscularian realism, and that *Siris* furnishes evidence of this change of heart.[18] However, corpuscularians attribute casual powers to material substance, and it's hard to construe any of Berkeley's writings as friendly to material causality. Certainly, Berkeley remained a scientific instrumentalist: 'The mechanical philosopher . . . inquires properly concerning the rules and modes of operation alone, and not concerning the cause; forasmuch as nothing mechanical is or really can be a *cause*' (*S* 249). Such unequivocal rejection of mechanical causation is hard to reconcile with corpuscularianism.[19]

In a more Berkeley-friendly spirit, Ian Hacking claims that learning how to interpret information from instruments is a useful model of Berkeley's *New Theory of Vision* (and one might add the Divine Language of Nature) in action. When we learn how to use instruments, we have to learn anew how to correlate the visual and tactile cues which we receive from the microscope and thus we can observe in action the process of synthesizing a perceptual world out of disparate cues:

> Tactile sense is correlated with our allegedly two-dimensional retinal image, and this learned cueing produces three-dimensional perception. . . . Whether or not Berkeley was right about primary vision, new ways of seeing, acquired after infancy, involve learning by doing, not just passive looking.[20]

Microscopy recapitulates visual learning in a form which adult percipients can observe first hand, but this time self-consciously.

In emphasising non-ideational uses of language and warning against our being misled by words, Berkeley has been acclaimed as a significant forerunner of Wittgenstein's later views of meaning-as-use and the 'Private Language Argument' attack on inner, ideational theories of meaning.[21] Berkeley was strikingly modern in insisting that the meaning of some terms is best uncovered by attending to the value given to these utterances in use, rather than explicating meanings in terms of reference to private objects. (In *Alciphron*, Berkeley expands on those non-ideational uses of language that involves exhorting or inspiring the hearer. Therein, Berkeley argues that theoretical terms in physical science are on identical footing to terms like 'grace' or 'the joys of the blessed' in Christian apologetics. Ideas cannot be formed of objects answering to any of these terms, yet they have a function and can still serve to convey a meaning.[22])

Dismaying as Berkeley would find this, orthodoxy in contemporary Western philosophy tends to materialist monism, often in a functionalist/behaviourist form. Although usually associated with materialist or physicalist views, neither behaviourism nor functionalism are substance monisms as such and might be combined with various metaphysical conceptions. However, the classical empiricist view of concept formation (i.e. that the scope of possible concept formation is restricted by the scope of possible sense-experience) has been almost overwhelmingly rejected since Berkeley's time. The decline of idealism in twentieth-century analytical philosophy has much to do with the rise of externalist and especially reliabilist positions in epistemology, coupled with that of metaphysical/semantic doctrines like content-externalism. Likewise, Moorean anti-sceptical strategies have drawn little direct inspiration from Berkeley's idealist anti-scepticism.[23] However, Berkeleyan idealism attracted the enthusiastic advocacy of such nineteenth- and twentieth-century Berkeley scholars as Alexander Campbell Fraser (1819–1914) and A. A. Luce (1882–1977). Indeed, versions of Berkeleyan idealism continue to be ingeniously and ably defended to this day.[24] So, the extent of Berkeley's influence goes far beyond those philosophers who looked to him for direct inspiration and encompasses a host of different philosophical positions and traditions.

CHAPTER 5

GUIDE TO FURTHER READING

Of the books already cited, I particularly recommend the following collections of articles:

1. John Foster and Howard Robinson (eds), *Essays on Berkeley: A Tercentennial Celebration* (Oxford, Clarendon, 1985).
2. Colin Murray Turbayne (ed.), *Berkeley: Critical and Interpretive Essays* (Manchester, Manchester University Press, 1982).
3. Kenneth P. Winkler (ed.), *The Cambridge Companion to Berkeley* (Cambridge, Cambridge University Press, 2005).

Likewise, of the individual books or monographs already cited, I particularly recommend:

1. David Berman, *George Berkeley: Idealism and the Man* (Oxford, Clarendon, 1994).
2. Kenneth P. Winkler, *Berkeley: An Interpretation* (Oxford, Clarendon, 1994).

The following suggestions aim to give a few ideas for ways of pursuing further some of the topics covered above.

BERKELEY'S LIFE

1. M. A. Stewart, 'Berkeley, George (1685–1753)', *Dictionary of National Biography* (Oxford, Oxford University Press, September 2004, on-line edition May 2005), Oxford Biography Index Number 101002211, available on-line at: www.oxforddnb.com/view/article/2211 [accessed 18 July 2008]. (Subscriber log-in required.)
2. Joseph Stock, 'An Account of the Life of George Berkeley, D. D., Late Bishop of Cloyne in Ireland' (London, J. Murray, 1776) available on-line at: www.maths.tcd.ie/~dwilkins/Berkeley/Stock/Life.html [accessed 18 July 2008].

3. J. O. Wisdom, 'An Outline of Berkeley's Life', *The British Journal for the Philosophy of Science*, vol. 4 (1953), pp. 78–87.

GENERAL ON BERKELEY AND THE *PRINCIPLES*

1. Jonathan Dancy, *Berkeley: An Introduction* (Oxford, Blackwell, 1987).
2. A. C. Grayling, *Berkeley: The Central Arguments* (London, Duckworth, 1986).
3. A. D. Ritchie, *George Berkeley: A Reappraisal* (New York, Manchester University Press/Barnes and Noble Inc., 1967).
4. John Wild, *George Berkeley* (Harvard, Harvard University Press, 1936).

STUDIES OF PARTICULAR BERKELEYAN ISSUES

1. Patrick Fleming, 'Berkeley's Immaterialist Account of Action', *Journal of the History of Philosophy*, vol. 44 (2006), pp. 415–29.
2. Richard T. Lambert, 'Berkeley's Commitment to Relativism', as in Turbayne (ed.), pp. 22–32.
3. William McGowan, 'Berkeley's Doctrine of Signs', as in Turbayne (ed.), pp. 231–46.
4. R. G. Muehlmann, *Berkeley's Ontology* (Indianapolis, Hackett, 1992).
5. Margaret D. Wilson, 'The Phenomenalisms of Leibniz and Berkeley', Ernest Sosa (ed.), *Essays on the Philosophy of George Berkeley* (Dordrecht, Holland, D. Reidel, 1987), pp. 3–22.
6. A. D. Woozley, 'Berkeley's Doctrine of Notions and Theory of Meaning', *Journal of the History of Ideas*, vol. 14 (1976), pp. 427–34.

THE NEW THEORY OF VISION

1. D. M. Armstrong, 'Berkeley's New Theory of Vision', *Journal of the History of Ideas*, vol. 17 (1956), pp. 127–9.
2. D. M. Armstrong, *Berkeley's Theory of Vision* (Melbourne, Melbourne University Press, 1960).
3. Thomas M. Lennon, 'Berkeley and the Ineffable', *Synthese*, vol. 75 (1988), pp. 231–50.
4. Thomas M. Lennon, 'The Genesis of Berkeley's *Theory of Vision Vindicated*', *History of European Ideas*, vol. 33 (2007), pp. 321–29.

5. Rolf Sartorius, 'A Neglected Aspect of the Relationship between Berkeley's Theory of Vision and his Immaterialism', *American Philosophical Quarterly*, vol. 6 (1969), pp. 318–23.

LOCKE AND BERKELEY ON ABSTRACT IDEAS, ETC.

1. James Farr, 'The Way of Hypotheses: Locke on Method', *Journal of the History of Ideas*, vol. 48 (1987), pp. 51–72, and reprinted in *Locke: Critical Assessments* (ed. Richard Ashcroft, London, Routledge, 1991), vol. 4, pp. 488–10.
2. Douglas Lewis, 'The Existence of Substances and Locke's Way of Ideas', *Theoria*, vol. 35 (1969), pp. 124–46 and reprinted in Ashcroft (ed.), vol. 4, pp. 79–96.
3. A. D. Woozley, 'Some Remarks on Locke's Account of Knowledge', *Locke Newsletter*, 2 (1972), pp. 7–17, and reprinted in *Locke on Human Understanding*, edited by I. C. Tipton, (Oxford, Oxford University Press, 1977), pp. 141–8.

BERKELEY ON MATERIAL SUBSTANCE

1. A. A. Luce, 'Berkeley's Existence in the Mind', *Mind*, New Series, vol. 50, no. 199 (1941), pp. 258–67.
2. A. A. Luce, *The Dialectic of Immaterialism: An Account of the Making of Berkeley's* Principles (London, Hodder and Stoughton, 1963).

BERKELEY'S PHILOSOPHY OF SCIENCE

1. Joseph Agassi, 'The Future of Berkeley's Instrumentalism: *Just Terrific as a Self-Observer*', *The Gentle Art of Philosophical Polemics* (La Salle, IL, Open Court, 1988), pp. 55–69.
2. Richard J. Brook, *Berkeley's Philosophy of Science* (Martinus Nijhoff, The Hague, 1973).

BERKELEY ON SPACE AND TIME

1. Robert Gray, 'Berkeley's Theory of Space', *Journal of the History of Philosophy*, vol. 16 (1978), pp. 415–34.
2. Gerard Hinrichs, 'The Logical Positivism of Berkeley's *De Motu*', *Review of Metaphysics*, vol. 3 (1950), pp. 491–505.
3. Gary Thrane, 'The Spaces of Berkeley's World', as in Turbayne (ed.), pp. 127–47.

NOTES

1. CONTEXT

1. *PC* were originally published as Berkeley's *Commonplace Book*, a title given to them by their first editor, Alexander Campbell Fraser and no longer widely used. See A. A. Luce, 'Berkeley's Philosophical Commentaries', *Mind* (New Series), vol. 59 (1950), p. 551. Given the wealth of Berkeley's marginal cross-references between *PC*-entries, always use an edition of *PC* that reprints his marginal signs.

2. *PC* is notable also for Berkeley's occasional barbed sally at his opponents, for example, 'There are men who say there are insensible extensions, there are others who say the Wall is not white, the fire is not hot &c We Irish men cannot attain to these truths' (*PC* 392). Alas for anyone who likes a good epigram, in published writings Berkeley followed his own advice: 'N.B. to rein in yʳ Satyrical nature', *PC* 634.

3. Berkeley's ordination as an Anglican priest followed in 1710. The rapidity of his progress from deacon to priest brought him sharp censure and a threat of prosecution from the then Archbishop of Dublin, William King. See David Berman, *George Berkeley: Idealism and the Man* (Oxford, Clarendon, 1994), pp. 17–20.

4. Cf. *PC* 508: 'the Being of a God & the Freedom of Man; these to be handled in the beginning of the Second Book'; for what might have gone into *PHK* Part III, see *PC* 583 and 853.

5. See David Berman's 'The Jacobitism of Berkeley's Passive Obedience', *Journal of the History of Ideas*, vol. 47 (1986), pp. 309–19, and also Berman, *George Berkeley*, pp. 82–97.

6. See *The Analyst, A Discourse Addressed to an Infidel Mathematician* (1734) and *A Defence of Freethinking in Mathematics* (1735), *Works* (Luce-Jessop edition), vol. IV.

7. The *apparent* artlessness of *S*'s design may be deliberate: 'In its fluid movement it can lead the modern reader only interested in the latest cure to consider divine subjects without his being aware of the transition', Peter Walmsley, *The Rhetoric of Berkeley's Philosophy* (Cambridge, Cambridge University Press, 1990), p. 145.

8. For more on early modern uses of 'idea', see Robert McRae, '"Idea" as a Philosophical Term in the Seventeenth Century', *Journal of the History of Ideas*, vol. 26 (1965), pp. 175–90. Cf. Douglas Greenlee, 'Locke's Idea of "Idea"', *Theoria*, vol. 33 (1967), pp. 98–106, reprinted in *Locke on Human Understanding*, edited by I. C. Tipton (Oxford, Oxford University Press, 1977), pp. 40–7, with discussion by Gunnar Aspelin (Tipton, pp. 47–51), and Greenlee's reply (Tipton, pp. 51–4).

9. In seventeenth-century terms, Locke and Berkeley were thus 'ideists', that is, believers that all direct objects of knowledge are ideas (cf. Luce, *Berkeley's Immaterialism: A Commentary on His 'A Treatise Concerning the Principles of Human Knowledge'* (London, Thomas Nelson and Sons, 1945), p. 25, fn. 2). John Sergeant attacked Locke's brand of ideism, in his *Solid Philosophy Asserted against the Fancies of the Ideists* (1697, facsimile of Locke's copy edited by Peter A. Schouls (New York, Garland, 1984)).

10. In a sense, abstract ideas stand to Berkeley's *PHK* rather as innate ideas do to Locke's *Essay*. Both works begin with wide-ranging attacks on an allegedly impossible and/or unnecessary form of ideas that they attribute to their opponents (Descartes in Locke's case, Locke in Berkeley's case). For Berkeley's attack on abstract ideas, see *PHK*, Introduction, *passim*. For Locke's attack on innate ideas (and principles), see *Essay* (I/iv).

11. See Jonathan Bennett, *Locke, Berkeley, Hume: Central Themes* (Oxford, Clarendon, 1971), pp. 14–20.

12. Cf. 'motion and impulse are properties of bodies and that therefore they can be found in objects and in our sense organs, but . . . the light and colors we see are modifications of the soul, which are quite different from the above properties and of which we also have quite different ideas', *Search*, 1.12.5.

13. See C. J. McCracken, *Malebranche and British Philosophy* (Oxford, Clarendon, 1983). Also, Anita Fritz, 'Malebranche and the Immaterialism of Berkeley', *Review of Metaphysics*, vol. 3 (1949–50), pp. 59–80.

14. 'God knows the nature of the soul because He finds in Himself a clear and representative idea of it. . . . But the soul is only darkness to itself; its light comes to it from elsewhere', *Search*, 4.11.3.

15. While Berkeley's differences with Malebranche were perfectly genuine, there may also be some politic exaggeration in Berkeley's distancing himself from Malebranche's doctrines. Espousing the doctrines of a Parisian Catholic priest was not a career-enhancing move for an Anglican clergyman c. 1710.

16. For these (and other) reasons, Harry Bracken argues that Berkeley was less a British empiricist and more an Irish Cartesian. See Bracken's *Berkeley* (London, Macmillan, 1974) and 'Berkeley: Irish Cartesian', *Philosophical Studies*, vol. 24 (1976), pp. 39–51. Tipton's review of Bracken (1974), (*Mind* (New Series), vol. 86 (1977), pp. 136–8) takes issue with Bracken. For a more Bracken-friendly account of Berkeley's Cartesianism, see Michael Ayers, 'Was Berkeley an Empiricist or a Rationalist?', in Kenneth P. Winkler (ed.), *The Cambridge Companion to Berkeley* (Cambridge, Cambridge University Press, 2005), pp. 34–62. At the very least, this debate does suggest how potentially misleading the empiricism/rationalism dichotomy can be when it comes to categorizing the great early modern philosophers.

2. OVERVIEW OF THEMES

1. See 'First Reactions' and 'Early Reviews', in C. J. McCracken and
   I. C. Tipton (eds), *Berkeley's Principles and Dialogues: Background
   Source Materials* (Cambridge, Cambridge University Press, 2000),
   pp. 159–72 and 173–90.
2. G. J. Warnock, *Berkeley* (Harmondsworth, Penguin, 1953), p. 17.
   For a similar account, see, for example, Alan Musgrave, *Common
   Sense, Science, and Scepticism: A Historical Introduction to the
   Theory of Knowledge* (Cambridge, Cambridge University Press,
   1993), p. 127.
3. James Boswell, *The Life of Samuel Johnson* (1791, Oxford, Oxford
   University Press, 1980), p. 333. N. B. Don't confuse Dr Samuel
   Johnson (1709–84) with Samuel Johnson (1696–1772), Berkeley's
   American philosophical correspondent and disciple.
4. Still, Dr Johnson did think Berkeley 'a profound scholar, as well as
   a man of fine imagination' (Boswell, *The Life of Samuel Johnson*,
   p. 448). Cf. 'Mr. Berkeley is a very ingenious man, and great philosopher', Jonathan Swift, *Journal to Stella*, Letter LXIII, 7 April
   1713, (Gloucester, Alan Sutton, 1984, p. 456).
5. Although Jean Brunet, French author of 'New Conjectures on
   the Sense Organs' (1686) and the now-lost *Projet d'une Nouvelle
   Métaphysique* (1703), may have (effectively or intentionally) been a
   solipsist. (See McCracken and I. C. Tipton (eds), *Berkeley's Principles and Dialogues*, pp. 70–6.) Brunet's contemporaries seemingly
   thought him a solipsist, and his remarks often have a solipsistic
   flavour. (E.g. 'One spreads oneself into all things and that, on
   a first and simple view of them, one doesn't distinguish oneself
   from them', ibid., p. 73.) Brunet anticipated Berkeley's 'Master
   Argument' (at *PHK* 22–3) that asserting that an object can exist
   without being thought of is self-contradictory. (Cf. 'Whatever
   exists is known; by that I mean that it would be contradictory to
   attribute a positive existence to something that one was not thinking of', ibid.) However, unlike Berkeley, Brunet doesn't seem to
   have distinguished sufficiently between existence outside the individual mind and existence outside the mind *tout court*, which might
   explain why Brunet seemed solipsistic to his contemporaries.
   Other, more minor differences 'twixt Berkeley and Brunet abound,
   for example, the latter accepted the possibility of an abstract idea
   of space and denied the reality of time as a succession of ideas.
6. However, the following denial is not one many Berkeley commentators would share: 'Therefore I take my courage in my two
   hands, and deny that Berkeley was an idealist', (A. A. Luce,
   Berkeley's Immaterialism, p. 25). Luce's use of idealist is idiosyn-
   cratic: 'I mean by idealism that type of philosophical doctrine
   found in the recognized idealists – Kant, Hegel and Bradley. If
   those three are idealists, then Berkley is not, and his teaching

can be assimilated to theirs only by being misrepresented' (ibid.). According to Luce, idealism *ought* to be a doctrine like materialism but with a different candidate for the fundamental stuff out of which reality is composed. As materialism sees everything as ultimately being composed of matter, so (Luce suggests) idealism should see everything as being composed ultimately of ideas. Berkeleyan idealism is *not* the doctrine that only ideas exist – besides ideas, there are also spiritual substances (or minds) that are not reducible to ideas or constructed from ideas.

7. Indeed, A. A. Luce (*Berkeley's Immaterialism*, p. 25) maintains that John Norris had a better title than Berkeley to being considered the 'English idealist of his day'. (For Norris, see McCracken and Tipton, *Berkeley's Principles and Dialogues*, pp. 132–41.)

8. Charlotte Johnston, 'Locke's Examination of Malebranche and John Norris', *Journal of the History of Ideas*, vol. 19 (1958), pp. 551–8.

9. For Collier, see McCracken and Tipton, *Berkeley's Principles and Dialogues*, pp. 142–56, and also Henry E. Allison, *Kant's Transcendental Idealism: An Interpretation and Defence* (New Haven, Yale University Press, 1983), p. 58. For the relationship between Berkeley and Collier, see G. A. Johnston, *The Development of Berkeley's Philosophy* (London, Macmillan, 1923), Appendix I, pp. 360–82.

3. READING THE TEXT

1. From a letter to Sir John Percival of 6 September 1710, reprinted in Benjamin Rand (ed.), *Berkeley and Percival: The Correspondence of George Berkeley, Afterwards Bishop of Cloyne, and Sir John Percival, Afterwards Earl of Egmont* (Cambridge, Cambridge University Press, 1914), p. 82.

2. 'My propositions serve as elucidations in the following way: anyone who understands me eventually recognises them as nonsensical, when he has used them – as steps – to climb up beyond them', Ludwig Wittgenstein, *Tractatus-Logico Philosophicus*, 6.54 (1922, trans. D. F. Pears and Brian McGuiness, London, Routledge and Kegan Paul, 1961). Although Berkeley clearly didn't think his own propositions were nonsensical, his aims were nonetheless therapeutic.

3. Cf. Descartes' answer to his own 'evil demon' scepticism. Having proved that God exists and that deception is not in the Divine nature in his third *Meditation*, Descartes concludes in his fourth *Meditation* that God would not have furnished us with senses only to have us eternally misled by an evil power, *Meditations on First Philosophy, with Selections from the Objections and Replies* (trans. and ed. John Cottingham, Cambridge, Cambridge University Press, 1986), pp. 37–43.

4. See J. L. Mackie, *Problems from Locke*, (Oxford, Oxford University Press, 1976), pp. 110–40.

5. For more details of the development of the view that Berkeley misconstrued Locke on abstract ideas and some objections to the 'misconstrual' view, see (among others):

- R. I. Aaron, 'Locke's Theory of Universals', *Proceedings of the Aristotelian Society*, vol. 33 (1933), pp. 173–202.
- Winston H. F. Barnes, 'Did Berkeley Misunderstand Locke?', *Mind*, New Series, vol. 49, no. 193 (1940), pp. 52–7.
- Monroe Beardsley, 'Berkeley on "Abstract Ideas"', *Mind*, New Series, vol. 52, no. 206 (1943), pp. 157–70.
- John Linnell, 'Locke's Abstract Ideas', *Philosophy and Phenomenological Research*, vol. 16 (1956), pp. 400–5.

6. At the height of his youthful particularism and anti-abstractionism, Berkeley seems to have toyed with the idea that mathematical truths are inherently abstractive and suspect. For instance, at one point he rejected Pythagoras Theorem but allowed squaring the circle: 'One square cannot be double of another. Hence the Pythagoric Theorem is false' (*PC* 500). In Berkeley's early particularism, squares and circles seem to be pointillist congeries of sensory ideas. If circles must contain determinate numbers of points, squares of the same area can always be constructed. Berkeley says of his opponents: 'I can square the circle &c they cannot, wch goes on the best principles' (*PC* 395).

7. This entry is marked '+', a symbol many commentators think signifies an entry Berkeley later disagreed with or decided to excise (see A. A. Luce, *Berkeley and Malebranche: A Study in the Origins of Berkeley's Thought*, Oxford, Clarendon Press, 1934, revised edition, 1967, p. x). While not all *PC* uses of '+' may indicate cancellation, this hypothesis fits better than any other so far proposed. For a thorough assessment of the '+' problem, see Robert McKim, 'Berkeley's Notebooks', in Winkler (ed.), *The Cambridge Companion*, pp. 63–93.

8. See, for example, *How to Do Things with Words: The William James Lectures delivered at Harvard University in 1955* (ed. J. O. Urmson, Oxford, Clarendon Press, 1962).

9. Cf. 'The human senses have had a much longer history than the human intellect, and have been brought much nearer to perfection: they are far more acute, far less easy to deceive', A. E. Housman, 'The Application of Thought to Textual Criticism' (*Collected Poems and Selected Prose*, ed. Christopher Ricks, Harmondsworth, Penguin, 1988), p. 329.

10. Locke accused the Schoolmen of creating: 'a curious and inexplicable Web of perplexed Words' (*Essay* III/x/8). Cf. Berkeley on 'the obscure subtlety of the Schoolmen, which for so many ages like some dread plague, has corrupted philosophy' (*DM* 40).

11. Cf. Locke on mistaking a humanly manufactured definition of the properties a substance contains for the actual powers residing in that substance (i.e. mistaking nominal essence for real

essence): 'Yet there is scarce any Body in the use of these Words, but often supposes each of those names to stand for a thing having the real Essence, on which those Properties depend' (*Essay* III/x/18).

12. Cf. *PC* 429: 'Existere is percipi or percipere ∧. The horse is in the stable, the Books are in the study as before'. To which is appended *PC* 429a: '∧ or velle i.e. agere'.

13. 'Past existence, future existence and possible existence are all relative to perception, and *absolute existence* is a mere limbo, an unintelligible concept' (Luce, *Berkeley's Immaterialism*, p. 60).

14. For more on the different senses of impossibility in Berkeley, see the following exchange:

    1. Peter S. Wenz, 'Berkeley's Christian Neo-Platonism', *Journal of the History of Ideas*, vol. 37 (1976), pp. 537–46.
    2. Robert McKim, 'Wenz on Abstract Ideas and Christian Neo-Platonism in Berkeley', *Journal of the History of Ideas*, vol. 43 (1982), pp. 665–71.
    3. Peter S. Wenz, 'Berkeley's Two Concepts of Impossibility: A Reply to McKim', *Journal of the History of Ideas*, vol. 43 (1982), pp. 673–80.

15. See Luce, *The Dialectic of Immaterialism: An Account of the Making of Berkeley's* Principles (London, Hodder and Stoughton, 1963), p. 71 and Pierre Bayle, *Historical and Critical Dictionary: Selections* (trans. Richard H. Popkin, Indianapolis, Hackett, 1991), pp. 350–88. See also Harry M. Bracken, 'Bayle, Berkeley and Hume', *Eighteenth Century Studies*, vol. 11 (1977–8), pp. 227–45. Berkeley mentions Bayle at *PC* 358 and 424, and at *TVV* 6.

16. Although the argument seems to be original to Bayle in its fundamentals. See Thomas M. Lennon, 'Pierre Bayle', *The Stanford Encyclopedia of Philosophy (Summer 2008)*, Edward N. Zalta (ed.), http://plato.stanford.edu/archives/sum2008/entries/bayle/ [accessed 18 July 2008].

17. Gideon Yaffe, 'Thomas Reid', *The Stanford Encyclopedia of Philosophy (Winter 2005)*, Edward N. Zalta (ed.), http://plato.stanford.edu/archives/win2005/entries/reid/, p. 8 [accessed 18 July 2008].

18. Stephan Blatti, 'Disjunctivism', *The Continuum Encyclopedia of British Philosophy*, ed. A. C. Grayling, Andrew Pyle and Naomi Goulder (London, Thoemmes Continuum, 2006, vol. 2, pp. 856–7), p. 856. (Also on-line at http://users.ox.ac.uk/~univ1741/documents/Grayling2.pdf [accessed 18 July 2008].)

19. M. G. F. Martin, 'The Transparency of Experience', *Mind & Language*, vol. 17 (2002), pp. 376–425. Draft on-line at: www.nyu.edu/gsas/dept/philo/courses/concepts/martin.html [accessed 18 July 2008].

20. Also known as the 'principle of parsimony' or the principle of ontological economy, Ockham's Razor is most often expressed as

'Entities are not to be multiplied beyond necessity' (or 'entia non sunt multiplicanda praeter necessitatem'). Named after the aforementioned English logician, philosopher, Franciscan and nominalist, William of Ockham, the Razor appears nowhere in the surviving works which bear his name and was seemingly first referred to under that name in the works of Sir William Hamilton (1805–65). The principle urges simplicity in assessing and evaluating explanations – use only the minimal number of entities or principles which will suffice for an explanation.

21. Andre Gallois, 'Berkeley's Master Argument', *The Philosophical Review*, vol. 83 (1974), pp. 55–69.
22. See James Franklin, 'David Stove's Discovery of the Worst Argument in the World', *Philosophy*, vol. 77 (2002), pp. 615–16.
23. G. Pitcher, *Berkeley* (London, Routledge, 1977), p. 113.
24. See Mackie, *Problems from Locke*, p. 54, fn. 19. For a similar but slightly more formal argument to a similar effect, that charges the 'Master Argument' with a kind of fallacy of composition, see also J. L. Mackie, 'Self-Refutation – A Formal Analysis', *The Philosophical Quarterly*, vol. 14 (1964), pp. 193–203, pp. 200–1.
25. 'Selections from the Correspondence with Clarke', *Leibniz: Philosophical Writings* (ed. G. H. R. Parkinson, trans. Mary Morris and G. H. R. Parkinson, Dent, London, 1973), p. 211.
26. The PSR in turn is derivable from Leibniz's *Principle of the Identity of Indiscernibles* (*PII*). The *PII* holds that that there are 'no purely extrinsic denominations', and that 'all things which are different must be distinguished in some way' ('On the Principle of Indiscernibles', ed. Parkinson, pp. 133–5). In effect, *PII* states that if there is no detectable way in which two putative states of affairs differ, then they are in fact one state of affairs and not two distinct ones at all.
27. 'A Specimen of Discoveries about Marvellous Secrets of Nature in General', in Parkinson (ed.), *Leibniz: Philosophical Writings*, p. 76.
28. That is, one 'according to which we indirectly (mediately) perceive material things, by directly (immediately) perceiving ideas, which are mind-dependent items. The ideas *represent* external material objects, and thereby allow us to perceive them', Lisa Downing, 'George Berkeley', *The Stanford Encyclopedia of Philosophy* (Winter 2007 Edition), ed. Edward N. Zalta, http://plato.stanford.edu/archives/win2007/entries/berkeley/, section 2.1.1, original emphasis [accessed 18 July 2008].
29. For representationalism in Locke and Malebranche, see H. E. Matthews, 'Locke, Malebranche and the Representative Theory', *Locke Newsletter* no. 2 (1971), pp. 12–21; reprinted in Tipton (ed., 1977), pp. 55–61.
30. A subtle defence of (at least some of) the assumptions behind the Master Argument can be found in Christopher Peacocke, 'Imagination, Experience and Possibility: A Berkelian View Defended', as in John Foster and Howard Robinson (eds), *Essays on*

Berkeley: A Tercentennial Celebration (Oxford, Clarendon, 1985), pp. 19–35. Peacocke argues that conception is necessarily from an implicit viewpoint.

31. On solipsism and Berkeley, see Dennis Grey, 'The Solipsism of Bishop Berkeley', *The Philosophical Quarterly*, vol. 2 (1952), pp. 338–49, and Robert J. Fogelin, *Routledge Philosophy Guidebook to Berkeley and the Principles of Human Knowledge* (London, Routledge, 2001), pp. 144–50.

32. See also Robinson, Introduction, pp. xxvii–xxxiii, on the links between the Master Argument and the attack on abstract ideas.

33. Cf. *PC* 577: 'The very existence of Ideas constitutes the soul', and *PC* 580: 'Mind is a Congeries of Perceptions. Take away perceptions and you take away the Mind put the perceptions and you put the mind'. (Both these entries are marked '+'.)

34. Descartes offers something like the common-sense riposte to dreaming scepticism, namely that waking life presents a coherence and an orderly succession of appearance, in stark contrast to the fragmentary perceptions we have in dreams: 'dreams are never linked by memory with all the other actions of life as waking experiences are', Cottingham, *Meditations*, Sixth Replies, p. 61.

35. See, for example, Christopher Priest's novels *A Dream of Wessex* (London, Faber, 1977) and *The Extremes* (London, Scribner, 1998; London, Gollancz, 2005).

36. For more on Molyneux and Berkeley's theory of vision, see Colin M. Turbayne, 'Berkeley and Molyneux on Retinal Images', *Journal of the History of Ideas*, vol. 16 (1955), pp. 339–55.

37. See Dummett's 'Realism', in *Truth and Other Enigmas* (Duckworth, 1993), pp. 145–65, and reprinted in Michael J. Loux (ed.), *Metaphysics: Contemporary Readings* (London, Routledge, 2001), pp. 459–78.

38. For a different view of how Berkeley might interpret the construction of physical objects, whereby physical objects are like the theoretical entities postulated by science, see James W. Cornman, 'A Reconstruction of Berkeley: Minds and Physical Objects as Theoretical Entities', *Ratio*, vol. 13 (1971), pp. 76–87.

39. See John Stuart Mill, *Examination of Sir William Hamilton's Philosophy*, Ch. XI (1865, *Collected Works of John Stuart Mill*, vol. IX, Toronto/London, University of Toronto Press/Routledge and Kegan Paul, 1979), note on p. 187.

40. See, for example, A. J. Ayer, 'Phenomenalism', *Proceedings of the Aristotelian Society*, vol. 47 (1947), pp. 163–96, and reprinted in Ayer's *Philosophical Essays* (London, Macmillan, 1954), pp. 125–66.

41. See also John W. Davis, 'Berkeley and Phenomenalism', *Dialogue*, vol. 1 (1962–3), pp. 67–80.

42. Malebranche and his critics, notably Antoine Arnauld (1602–94), debated how, if at all, ideas are distinct from perceptions. See, for example, Andrew Pyle, *Malebranche* (London, Routledge, 2003), Ch. 4, pp. 74–95 and Tad Schmaltz, 'Nicolas Malebranche',

The Stanford Encyclopedia of Philosophy (Summer 2006 Edition), Edward N. Zalta (ed.), http://plato.stanford.edu/archives/sum2006/entries/malebranche/ [accessed 18 July 2008].

43. Hume took up the challenge of explaining why we think that the objects we perceive persist when we aren't perceiving them. As with induction or causation, Hume concluded that this is yet another case where our beliefs can only be explained by reference to psychological habit and not reasoning. See *Treatise*, I, IV, 2.

44. A saying that T. E. Jessop traces to Italian philosopher Agostino Nifo, or Augustinus Niphus, c. 1478–c. 1538. Berkeley probably found this slogan in the *De Augmentis Scientiarum* (5.4) of Sir Francis Bacon (1561–1626). See Robinson edition of *Principles*, note on *Principles* §51, p. 217.

45. See Majid Falchry, *Islamic Occasionalism* (London, Allen and Unwin, 1958), pp. 72–8. Malebranche cites ibn Gabirol (using the Latin rendering of the latter's name as 'Avicebron'), at the Fifteenth Elucidation of *Search*, see Lennon and Olscamp, p. 659. According to Malebranche, ibn Gabirol denied that material objects could exert causal powers on each other but allowed that 'minds are capable of acting on bodies because only they can penetrate them' (ibid.).

46. The great modern treatment of the problem of furnishing truth-conditions for counterfactual conditionals is David Lewis' *Counterfactuals* (Oxford, Blackwell, 1973), which uses an intricate semantics and metaphysics of possible worlds to analyse counterfactuals. For pre-Lewisian, non-possible-worlds, accounts of counterfactual conditionals, see, for example, Roderick M. Chisholm, 'The Contrary-to-Fact Conditional', *Mind*, vol. 55 (1946), pp. 289–307, and Nelson Goodman, 'The Problem of Counterfactual Conditionals', *The Journal of Philosophy*, vol. 44 (1947), pp. 113–28 (reprinted in Goodman's *Fact, Fiction and Forecast* (Cambridge, MA and London, Harvard University Press, 4th edition, 1983)), pp. 3–27.

47. See also discussion in Aaron Garrett, *Berkeley's Three Dialogues: A Reader's Guide* (London, Continuum, 2008), pp. 116–17. Garrett's guide is a volume I highly recommend.

48. *Micrographia, or Some Physiological Descriptions of Minute Bodies, Made by Magnifying Glasses with Some Observations and Inquiries Thereupon* (1665, facsimile edition, New York, Dover, 1961), Preface, p. xiv.

49. David Berman, 'Cognitive Theology and Emotive Mysteries in Berkeley's Alciphron', in David Berman (ed.), *Alciphron: In Focus* (London, Routledge and Kegan Paul, 1993), pp. 200–13.

50. '*Inference to the best explanation (IBE)*: reasoning from the fact that a hypothesis is the best available explanation of some evidence or belief to the fact that it is probably true', Adam Morton, *A Guide through the Theory of Knowledge* (Oxford, Blackwell, 2nd edition, 1997), p. 223.

51. David Hume, *Dialogues Concerning Natural Religion* and *The Natural History of Religion* (ed. J. C. A. Gaskin, Oxford, Oxford University Press, 1993). Cf. 'As every enquiry, which regards religion, is of the utmost importance, there are two questions in particular, which challenge our attention, to wit that concerning its foundation in reason and, and that concerning its origin in human nature' (ibid., p. 134). Hume's *Natural History* laid a distinctive emphasis on the second question.

52. For a very detailed account of Berkeley's theory of notions and meaning, see Daniel Flage, *Berkeley's Doctrine of Notions: A Reconstruction Based on His Theory of Meaning* (New York, St Martin's, 1987).

53. Cf. 'Berkeley and Hume . . . only thought of *qualities*, and altogether ignored *relations* as universals', Bertrand Russell, *The Problems of Philosophy* (Oxford, Oxford University Press, 1912), p. 55.

54. The Socinians (named after uncle and nephew, Laelius and Faustus Socinus, 1525–62 and 1539–1604 respectively) were an Antitrinitarian sect, mainly active in the sixteenth and seventeenth centuries, who denied the divinity of Jesus and held that the Son of God did not exist before being born as a human being.

55. Peter Unger, 'I Do Not Exist', *Perception and Identity*, ed. G. F. MacDonald (London, Macmillan, 1979).

56. Cf. St Augustine on the familiarity of time disappearing once time is considered in the abstract or in its own nature, *Confessions* (trans. Henry Chadwick, Oxford, Oxford University Press, 1998), Book XI, 'Time and Eternity', pp. 221–45.

57. See also E. J. Furlong, 'On Being "Embrangled" by Time', Colin Murray Turbayne (ed.), *Berkeley: Critical and Interpretive Essays* (Manchester University Press, 1982), pp. 148–55.

58. 'Although Newton himself was no infidel, the Newtonian system was a powerful influence on those who regarded the universe simply as a gigantic machine, and Berkeley was therefore anxious to undermine Newton's authority', G. J. Whitrow, 'Berkeley's Philosophy of Motion', *British Journal for the Philosophy of Science*, vol. 4 (1953), pp. 37–45, p. 37. For more on the Newton/Berkeley relationship, see also:

- John W. Davis, 'Berkeley, Newton and Space', *The Methodological Heritage of Newton*, ed. Robert E. Butts and John W. Davis (Toronto, University of Toronto Press, 1970), pp. 57–73.
- D. J. Greene, 'Smart, Berkeley, the Scientists and the Poets: A Note on Eighteenth Century Anti-Newtonianism', *Journal of the History of Ideas*, vol. XIV (1953), pp. 327–52.
- M. Hughes, 'Newton, Hermes and Berkeley', *British Journal for the Philosophy of Science*, vol. 43 (1992), pp. 1–19.
- W. A. Suchting, 'Berkeley's Criticism of Newton on Space and Motion', *Isis*, vol. 58 (1967), pp. 186–97.

Notes

NOTES

59. See, for example, Barry Gower's *Scientific Method: An Historical and Philosophical Introduction* (London, Routledge, 1997), Ch. 4, pp. 40–62.
60. Richard Slobodin's biography of anthropologist and psychiatrist, W. H. R. Rivers, cites *PHK* 105 as a guide to scientific empiricism: 'How firmly Rivers is in British empiricist tradition may be confirmed by noting Bishop Berkeley's distinction between natural philosophers, i.e. scientists, and other men', *W. H. R. Rivers* (2nd edition, Gloucester, Alan Sutton, 1997), pp. 114–5, fn. 1.
61. Cf. Newton, 'For all the difficulty of philosophy seems to consist in this, from the phenomena of motions to investigate the forces of nature, and then from these forces to demonstrate the other phenomena', H. G. Alexander (ed.), *The Leibniz-Clarke Correspondence* (Manchester, University of Manchester Press, 1956), p. 144.
62. *Principia Mathematica*, Scholium to Definition VIII (taken from Alexander, *The Leibniz-Clarke Correspondence*, p. 170).
63. For example, 'the forces of receding from the axis of circular motion', Newton, *Principia Mathematica* (trans. Andrew Motte, rev. Florian Cajori, Berkeley, University of California, 1966), vol. 1, p. 10.
64. For an admirably clear account of the bucket experiment, see Barry Dainton, *Time and Space* (Chesham, Acumen, 2001), pp. 173–4.
65. See Whitrow, 'Berkeley's Philosophy of Motion' and Karl Popper, 'A Note on Berkeley as Precursor of Mach and Einstein', *The British Journal for the Philosophy of Science*, vol. 4 (1953), pp. 26–36, reprinted in Popper's *Conjectures and Refutations* (London, Routledge and Kegan Paul, 5th edition, 1989), pp. 166–74.
66. Mach, *The Science of Mechanics* (6th edition, trans. Thomas J. McCormack, Open Court, La Salle, IL, 1960), p. 284. Einstein later derived the identity of gravitational and inertial mass from Mach's suggestion that inertial effects could be due, not to absolute motion, but to the gravitation of distant bodies.
67. See, for example, Max Black, 'Achilles and the Tortoise', *Analysis*, vol. 11 (1951), pp. 91–101.
68. The targets of these remarks might include Neoplatonic philosophers, Nicolas of Cusa and Galileo. See Woolhouse edition of *Principles* and *Dialogues*, p. 214, n. 75.
69. For more on actual versus potential infinity, see A. W. Moore, *The Infinite* (London, Routledge, 2nd edition, 2001), pp. 39–40, and for more on Berkeley's criticism of mathematical infinity, see ibid., pp. 65–6.
70. Cf. 'I do not think that if each pebble were broken into a million pieces the difficulty of getting over the road would necessarily have increased; and I don't see why it should if one of these millions – or all of them – had been multiplied into an infinity',

175

C. S. Peirce (quoted in Black, 'Achilles and the Tortoise', p. 101, fn. 5).

71. The targets of this remark are Newton's and Leibniz's systems of calculus. See, for example, J. O. Wisdom's:

- 'The *Analyst* Controversy: Berkeley's Influence on the Development of Mathematics', *Hermathena*, vol. 29 (1939), pp. 3–29.
- 'The *Analyst* Controversy: Berkeley as Mathematician', *Hermathena*, vol. 59 (1942), pp. 111–28.
- 'Berkeley's Criticism of the Infinitesimal', *The British Journal for the Philosophy of Science*, vol. 4 (1953), pp. 22–5.

See also Geoffrey Cantor, 'Berkeley's *The Analyst* Revisited', *Isis*, vol. 75 (1984), pp. 668–83. For more on Berkeley's view of fluxions, see Douglas M. Jesseph, *Berkeley's Philosophy of Mathematics* (Chicago, University of Chicago Press, 1993), pp. 143–51.

72. Here, Berkeley seems to have in mind the Dutch mathematician Bernard Nieuwentijt – see Ben Vermeulen, 'Berkeley and Nieuwentijt on Infinitesimals', *Berkeley Newsletter*, no. 8, pp. 1–7.

73. Infinitesimals whose squares, cubes or higher powers are all equal to zero, are called 'nilpotent' by modern mathematicians. Such infinitesimals actually have well-defined uses in modern mathematics. See, for example, Anders Kock, 'Differential Calculus and Nilpotent Real Numbers', *The Bulletin of Symbolic Logic*, vol. 9 (2003), pp. 225–30.

74. Margaret Atherton, *Berkeley's Revolution in Vision* (Ithaca, Cornell University Press, 1990), p. 116. See also Atherton, 'Berkeley's Revolution in Vision and its Reception', in Winkler (ed.), *The Cambridge Companion*, pp. 94–124 and David Raynor, '*Minima Sensibilia* in Berkeley and Hume', *Dialogue* (Canada), vol. 19 (1980), pp. 196–200.

75. See Ludwig Wittgenstein, *Philosophical Investigations* (trans. G. E. M. Anscombe, 3rd edition, Oxford, Blackwell, 1967), Part I, sections 243–315.

76. René Descartes, *Selected Philosophical Writings* (trans. John Cottingham, Robert Stoothoff and Dugald Murdoch, Cambridge, Cambridge University Press, 1988), p. 74.

77. Richard Swinburne, 'Personal Identity: The Dualist Theory', as in Loux (ed.) (2001, pp. 420–46), pp. 442–3.

78. In his *The Great Christian Doctrine of Original Sin Defended* (1758) (ed. Clyde A. Holbrook, New Haven, CT, Yale University Press, 1970).

79. R. M. Chisholm, 'Identity through Time', *Language, Belief and Metaphysics* (ed. H. Keifer and M. Munitz, 1970), and reprinted in *Metaphysics: The Big Questions* (ed. Dean Zimmerman and Peter van Inwagen, Oxford, Blackwell, 1998, pp. 173–85, p. 184). See also Clyde A. Holbrook, 'Jonathan Edwards Addresses Some "Modern Critics" of Original Sin', *The Journal of Religion*, vol. 63 (1983), pp. 211–30.

80. See C. C. W. Taylor, 'Action and Inaction in Berkeley', as in Foster and Robinson (eds), pp. 211–25.
81. See also A. David Kline, 'Berkeley's Divine Language Argument', in Ernest Sosa (ed.), *Essays on George Berkeley* (Dordrecht, Holland, D. Reidel) and reprinted in Berman (ed.), *Alciphron*, pp. 185–99.
82. Malebranche, *Dialogues on Metaphysics*, First Dialogue, Part X, quoted from *Philosophical Selections* (ed. Steven Nadler, Indianapolis, IN, Hackett, 1992), p. 157.
83. D. M. Armstrong, *What is a Law of Nature?* (Cambridge, Cambridge University Press, 1975), p. 105.
84. Cf. Berkeley on the possibility of God's suspending a general law to avert a particular, local evil: 'Suppose a Prince, on whose Life the Welfare of a Kingdom depends, to fall down a Precipice, we have no Reason to think, that the Universal Law of Gravitation wou'd be suspended in that Case. The like may be said of all other laws of Nature, which we do not find to admit of Exceptions on particular Accounts' (*Passive Obedience*, section 27, p. 27 of 1712 edition). (Also cited in Berman, 'The Jacobitism of Berkeley's Passive Obedience', p. 314.)

4. RECEPTION AND INFLUENCE

1. The 'early reader' in question was no less a person than Leibniz, and the comment quoted above was made in a letter to Bartholomew des Bosses (quoted here from McCracken and Tipton (eds), *Berkeley's Principles and Dialogues*, p. 191). While Leibniz too rejected absolute space and thought that all existence was mental (strictly, all existent substances are perceivers in Leibniz's system), he nonetheless differed from Berkeley on abstract ideas, the calculus and infinite divisibility. (See ibid. p. 192.)
2. See Hume's brief autobiography 'My Own Life', reprinted in Gaskin (ed.), *Dialogues*, pp. 3–10 (quotation from p. 5).
3. See, for example, Reid's *Essays on the Intellectual Powers of Man* (1785), Chs 10 and 11, as in *Essays on the Intellectual Powers of Man: A Critical Edition* (ed. Derek Brookes and Knud Haakonssen, Pennsylvania, Penn State Press, 2002).
4. See William James, *Pragmatism: In Focus* (1907, ed. Doris Olin, London, Routledge, 1993), pp. 55–6.
5. 'The one intelligible theory of the universe is that of objective idealism, that matter is effete mind, inveterate habits becoming physical laws', C. S. Peirce, 'The Architecture of Theories', *The Monist*, vol. 1 (1891), pp. 161–76, and reprinted in *Chance, Love, and Logic: Philosophical essays* (ed. Morris R. Cohen, Lincoln, NE, University of Nebraska Press, 1998, pp. 157–78) (1998 edition, pp. 169–70).
6. Although to what extent Hume's philosophy of topics like abstraction was informed by close study of Berkeley remains

controversial. See, for example, the following exchange:

1. Philip P. Wiener, 'Did Hume Ever Read Berkeley?', *The Journal of Philosophy*, vol. 56 (1959), pp. 533–5.
2. Richard H. Popkin, 'Did Hume Ever Read Berkeley?', *The Journal of Philosophy*, vol. 56 (1959), pp. 535–45.
3. Ernest Campbell Mossner, 'Did Hume Ever Read Berkeley? A Rejoinder to Professor Popkin', *The Journal of Philosophy*, vol. 56 (1959), pp. 992–5.
4. Richard H. Popkin, 'So, Hume Did Read Berkeley', *The Journal of Philosophy*, vol. 61 (1964), pp. 773–8.

7. Compare Russell's talk of material objects as 'unsensed sensibilia', in his neutral monist phase when he defined matter as any external cause of sensa. See Russell's 'On the Nature of Acquaintance II: Neutral Monism', *The Monist*, vol. 24 (1914), pp. 161–87. The link between idealism and neutral monism is strong: 'Neutral monism is regarded by some as an idealistic doctrine in which both sensations and physical elements are conscious sensations', E. C. Banks, 'The Philosophical Roots of Ernst Mach's Economy of Thought', *Synthese*, vol. 139 (2004), pp. 23–53, p. 50, fn. 77.

8. Mill, *Examination of Sir William Hamilton's Philosophy*, Ch. XII, Appendix, note on p. 205.

9. J. L. Austin, *Sense and Sensibilia* (Oxford, Oxford University Press, 1962), p. 132–42.

10. See, for example, Kant, *The Critique of Pure Reason* (trans. Norman Kemp Smith, London, Macmillan, 1929), A (1781) 165, B (1787) 208.

11. 'To use a very crude analogy, space and time are the spectacles through which our eyes are affected by objects. The spectacles are irremovable. Objects can be seen only through them. Objects, therefore, can never be seen as they are in themselves', Stephan Körner, *Kant* (Harmondsworth, Penguin, 1955), p. 37.

12. See A. C. Ewing (ed.), *The Idealist Tradition: From Berkeley to Blanshard* (Glencoe, IL, Free Press, 1957). For a modern statement and defence of Hegelian-inspired idealism, see T. L. S. Sprigge (1932–2007), *The Vindication of Absolute Idealism* (Edinburgh, Edinburgh University Press, 1983).

13. See N. M. L. Nathan, 'McTaggart's Immaterialism', *The Philosophical Quarterly*, vol. 41 (1991), pp. 442–56.

14. J. M. E. McTaggart, 'The Unreality of Time', *Mind* (New Series), vol. 17 (1908), pp. 457–74.

15. Cf. 'If Satan may rebuke sin, Kant may refute idealism' (Luce, *Berkeley's Immaterialism*, p. 26).

16. Nancy Cartwright, *Nature's Capacities and Their Measurement* (Oxford University Press, 1989), p. 3.

17. Ibid. The Glanvill quotation can be found in Joseph Glanvill, *The Vanity of Dogmatizing: The Three Versions* (facsimile of 1661 edition, Hove, Harvester Press, 1970), pp. 6–7.

18. See Gabriel Moked, *Particles and Ideas: Bishop Berkeley's Corpuscularian Philosophy* (Oxford, Clarendon, 1988).
19. For more on the continuity of Berkeley's philosophy of science, see Lisa Downing, 'Berkeley's Natural Philosophy and Philosophy of Science' (Winkler (ed.), *The Cambridge Companion*), pp. 230–65.
20. Ian Hacking, *Representing and Intervening* (Cambridge, Cambridge University Press 1983), p. 189.
21. See Antony Flew, 'Was Berkeley a Precursor of Wittgenstein?', in W. B. Todd (ed.), *Hume and the Enlightenment: Essays Presented to Ernest Campbell Mossner* (Edinburgh, Edinburgh University Press, 1974), and reprinted in Berman (ed.), *Alciphron*, pp. 214–26.
22. See *Alciphron*, Dialogue Seven, sections 5–7 (Berman edition, pp. 125–7).
23. See, for example, G. E. Moore, 'The Refutation of Idealism', *Mind* (New Series), vol. 12 (1903), pp. 433–53.
24. John Foster defends an essentially Berkeleyan form of idealism in *The Case for Idealism* (London, Routledge and Kegan Paul, 1982).

INDEX

qualities (Primary and
secondary) 6–7, 8, 42–3, 44–6,
47, 48–9, 50, 86, 105, 116
qualities (Tertiary) 48–9

rationalism/rationalist 10, 32,
50, 62, 156, 158, 166 *see also*
Descartes, René
realism (about universals) *see*
universals
realism (direct) 34, 36, 77
realism (indirect) 43, 92
Reid, Thomas (1710–96)
155–6, 170, 177
relationalism (about space)
127–31, 154 *see also* absolutism
(about space); Newton's
bucket experiment
relations 17, 22, 28, 30, 42, 46,
47, 49, 52, 70, 80, 101, 115, 124,
129, 144, 151, 174
relations, (mind-dependence of)
101, 115, 129
representationalism 4, 9, 34–5,
44, 49, 53, 54, 62, 75, 155, 171
Robinson, Howard x, 63–4, 84,
162, 172, 173
Russell, Bertrand (1872–1970)
115, 178

sceptic/scepticism 7, 9, 10, 12,
13, 14, 21, 22–3, 43–4, 53, 59,
64, 79, 100, 111, 113–14, 116,
117, 119, 120, 124, 140, 142,
144, 145, 151, 154, 155, 156,
161, 168, 172
Scholasticism 7, 29, 30–1, 32, 82,
86, 120, 121–2, 169
Schoolmen *see* Scholasticism
science ix, 2, 3, 21, 41, 87, 90,
93, 95–7, 99, 113, 119–22, 124,
125–7, 131, 148, 151, 157, 159,
160, 164, 172, 174, 175, 179
Search After Truth (Malebranche)
xiii, 166, 173
sense data 82, 83, 115
senses (additional/ extra) 107,
109, 140

Sergeant, John (1622–1707) 166
Shaftesbury (3rd Earl), Anthony
Ashley Cooper 1671–1713 3
Siris (1744) xii, 3, 159
Socinianism 117, 174
solipsism 15–16, 63, 142, 146,
167, 172
soul/spirit 2, 11, 15, 19, 34, 36,
37, 38, 40, 55, 68–9, 70, 71, 73,
75, 77, 85, 88–9, 92, 95, 106,
108, 109, 113–16, 118, 122, 139,
140–1, 143–5, 146–7, 166,
168, 172
space 2, 100, 125, 127–32, 151,
154, 156, 158, 164, 167, 174,
177, 178
space, (deification of) 131
Spinoza, Baruch (1632–77) 131
Sprigge, T. L. S. (1932–2007) 178
square circle 40, 43, 140
Stove, David (1927–94) 59, 171
substance (general) 4–5, 7, 8, 9,
11–12, 18–19, 54–5, 92, 100, 103,
104–5, 106, 107–8, 109, 116, 119,
139, 160–1, 164, 169–70
substance (material) 6, 13,
17–19, 31, 43–5, 46, 48, 49–50,
51, 53, 54, 56, 57, 63, 65,
74–8, 79, 85, 88, 92, 99–100,
112, 114, 116, 119, 129, 139,
140, 150, 155, 156, 159, 164
see also materialism; Master
Argument
substance (mental) 4, 11, 12, 19,
39, 40–1, 43, 45, 52, 68, 70, 75,
79, 88, 90, 91, 100, 101–2, 112,
114, 116, 119, 139, 143–5, 168,
177 *see also* soul/spirit
substratum 14, 18, 38, 39, 41–2,
45, 49, 51, 53, 75, 78–9, 88, 101,
105, 107–8, 109, 110, 134 *see
also* substance
Swift, Jonathan (1667–1745)
13–14, 167
Swinburne, Richard 176

teleological explanations/
argument 121, 124

theism/theist 55, 67, 84, 94, 96, 98, 104, 124, 132, 139, 150, 153, 157 *see also* deism/deist

Three DialoguesBetween Hylas and Philonous (1710) x, xii, 2, 10, 13, 31, 37, 41, 45, 59, 73, 84, 97, 108, 124, 139, 141, 155, 173

time 100, 112, 117–18, 119, 126, 144, 158, 164, 167, 174, 178

Treatise of Human Nature, A (David Hume) xiii, 68, 145, 155, 156, 173

triangle (abstract idea) 5, 26, 28–30

Trinity College, Dublin 1, 2

universals 22, 25, 27–8, 115, 126, 135, 144, 169, 174 *see also* abstract ideas

Vanity of Dogmatizing, The see Glanvill, Joseph

virtual reality 74

Wittgenstein, Ludwig (1889–1951) 23, 142, 160, 168, 176, 179

Woolhouse, Roger x, 72, 175

'Worst Argument in the World, The' *see* Stove, David

Zeno of Elea (fl. c. 475 BC) 45, 132, 138